INDIVIDUAL, FAMILY, COMMUNITY:

JUDEO-PSYCHOLOGICAL PERSPECTIVES

INDIVIDUAL
FAMILY
COMMUNITY

*Judeo-Psychological
Perspectives*

by

REUVEN P. BULKA

Author of the Coming Cataclysm

MOSAIC PRESS
Oakville – New York – London

CANADIAN CATALOGUING IN PUBLICATION DATA

Bulka, Reuven P.
 Inividual, family, community : Judeo-psychological
perspectives

Bibliography: p.
Includes index.
ISBN 0-88962-377-5 (bound). ISBN 0-88962-378-3 (pbk.)

1. Sociology, Jewish. 2. Judaism and psychology.
I. Title.

HN40.J5B84 1988   296.3'8783   C88-094816-7

Published by MOSAIC PRESS, P.O. Box 1032, Oakville, Ontario, L6J
5E9, Canada. Offices and warehouse at 1252 Speers Road, Units# 1&2,
Oakville, Ontario, L6L 5N9, Canada.

Mosaic Press acknowledges the assistance of the Canada Council and
the Ontario Arts Council in support of its publishing programme.

Copyright©Reuvin P. Bulka, 1989.
Design by Rita Vogel
Typeset by Aztext Electronics Publishing Ltd.

Printed and bound in Canada.

ISBN 0-88962-385-6 PAPER
ISBN 0-88962-386-4 CLOTH

MOSAIC PRESS:
In Canada:
      MOSAIC PRESS, 1252 Speers Road, Units# 1&2, Oakville,
Ontario L6J 5N9, Canada. P.O. Box 1032, Oakville, Ontario L6J 5E9

In the United States:
      Riverrun Press Inc., 1170 Broadway, Suite 807, New York, N.Y.,
10001, U.S.A., distributed by Kampmann & Co., 9 East 40th Street,
New York, N.Y., 10016

In the U.K.:
      John Calder (Publishers) Ltd., 18 Brewer Street, London, W1R
4A5, England.

INDIVIDUAL, FAMILY, COMMUNITY
Judeo-Psychological Perspectives

by Reuven P. Bulka

IN LOVING MEMORY
   of a dear Uncle

   MAX ALT

Unswerving in his faith
Heroic in resistance of Nazi brutality
Humble in the face of his heroism
Exemplary in his devotion to family

ACKNOWLEDGEMENTS

Among the chapters that comprise this volume, some are adapted from, and others are expanded versions of articles that have previously appeared in various journals. Gratitude is expressed to the editors and publishers of the following for their gracious permission to publish those articles in the present volume.

"Death in Life," from *Humanitas: Journal of the Institute of Man* (now Studies in Formative Spirituality), February 1974, 10 (1), pp. 33-41. Published by Institute of Formative Spirituality, Duquesne University, Pittsburgh, Pennsylvania, 15282.

"Rabbinic Attitudes to Suicide," from *Midstream*, October 1979, 23 (8), pp. 43-49. Published by Theodor Herzl Foundation, 515 Park Avenue, New York, New York, 10022.

"Honesty vs. Hypocrisy," from *Judaism*, Spring 1976, 23 (2), pp. 209-216. Published by American Jewish Congress, 15 East 84th Street, New York, New York, 10028.

"The Role of the Individual in Jewish Law," from *Tradition*, Spring- Summer 1973, 13 (4) - 14 (1), pp. 124-136. Published by Rabbinical Council of America, 275 Seventh Avenue, New York, New York, 10001.

"The Family: A Jewish Trouble Spot," from *Jewish Life*, 1982, pp. 25-34. Published by Union of Orthodox Jewish Congregations of America, 45 West 36th Street, New York, New York, 10018.

REUVEN P. BULKA

"Women's Role: Some Ultimate Concerns," from *Tradition*, Spring 1979, 17 (4), pp. 27-40. Published by Rabbinical Council of America, 275 Seventh Avenue, New York, New York, 10001.

"Divorce: The Problem and the Challenge," from *Tradition*, Summer 1976, 16 (1), pp. 127-133. Published by Rabbinical Council of America, 275 Seventh Avenue, New York, New York, 10001.

"Towards a Psychologically Sound Judaism," from *Journal of Psychology and Judaism*, Fall 1976, 1 (1), pp. 3-13. Published by Human Sciences Press, 72 Fifth Avenue, New York, New York, 10011.

"The Psychology of Conversion," from *Midstream*, October 1983, 29 (8),1, pp. 32-35. Published by Theodor Herzl Foundation, 515 Park Avenue, New York, New York, 10022.

"Psychoanalyzing the Nazis," from *Tradition*, Summer 1981, 19 (2), pp. 171-181. Published by Rabbinical Council of America, 275 Seventh Avenue, New York, New York, 10001.

Additionally, special thanks are extended to Blanche Osterer, whose preparation of the manuscript was instrumental in making this volume possible.

The helpfulness and cooperativeness of Howard Aster of Mosaic Press are greatly valued. Thanks too, to Rita Vogel. And, as always, the superb proofreading by my dear wife, Naomi, has been a significant help. To her, as well as the others who made this book possible, go my deep appreciation.

Reuven P. Bulka

INTRODUCTION

Judaism has bestowed on the world some of its most noble values. It is a unique value-expression with a particular perspective on the issues of the day, whether that day be the medieval period, the era of emancipation, modern times, or the future.

Judaism has proven itself quite adaptable to the contemporary idiom, be it in the theological or philosophical context. Today, the psychological idiom occupies center stage. The coalition of psychology and Judaism, whether it is to sharpen points of divergence or areas of convergence, is of concern to many leading thinkers. A *Journal of Psychology and Judaism*, a *Psychology-Judaism Reader*, numerous books and countless articles of modern vintage, all testify to this concern.

The issues addressed in this volume are divided into three categories - the individual, the family, and the community. Families are made up of individuals, communities are made up of families. Hence the division is more artificial than real. But the personal, the familial, and the communal, though interrelated, still comprise differing dimensions, different enough to justify the division.

To the individual, the issue of "To be or not to be" remains the question. The first chapters deal with attitude to death and suicide, gut issues of a "To be or not to be" nature. From "To be or not to be" we move to the question of "how to be." This is the focus of the next three chapters, dealing with loneliness, honesty, hypocrisy, and the individual's role and responsibility in the Judaic context.

The family, as the foundation stone of society, is going through a period of crisis and adjustment. The Jewish family, very much a part of society, is not immune to societal trends. These issues are examined in the first article of the second section. The changing role of women and its affect on the family is the second area of study, followed by a proposal concerning divorce which, though directed at the Jewish situation, is not without relevance to the larger community.

Finally, the third section, on communal concerns, approaches matters of particular importance to the Jewish community, with attendant concern for others. The state of Judaism is the agenda for the first two articles of this section. The first piece suggests the parameters for a psychologically sound Judaism, the second devotes itself to the state of the Rabbinate, or, in simple terms, the state of the "shapers" of modern Jewish reality. The concluding pieces deal with polar opposites, those who want to join Jewish ranks, and those who set out to destroy Jews and Judaism. A psychological perspective on the Jewish attitude to converts is proposed and then a Judaic perspective on the psychological study of the Nazis is imposed.

The theme of concern for the individual, the family, and society unifies the essays in this volume. This integration has been true of the Judaism of yesterday, continues in the present, and will hopefully set the tone for the collective future.

Reuven P. Bulka

SECTION ONE

THE INDIVIDUAL

CHAPTER 1

DEATH IN LIFE

In spite of all the sophistication of a highly technologized 20th century, we have still not come to grips with the psychologically traumatic and emotionally enervating experience of death. To be sure, one finds the odd intellectual or the odd ordinary person who is philosophical about death, who is ready, so to say, to live with death. However, the average person still fears death, the process of dying, and the experiencing of death. Perhaps it should be this way. It may be ridiculous for philosophers and psychologists to attempt pseudo-explanations which explain, even explain away, death. Perhaps it is the height of obscenity to reduce what is assuredly an awesome reality into an acceptable experience.

Upon reflection, it may be self-contradictory for one to glorify life and accept death at one and the same time. After all, if life is so valuable, and human existence so beautiful, death should be avoided. Even though death cannot be avoided in fact, it may be avoided in consciousness. Taking into consideration one's preoccupation with life, it is to be expected that thoughts of death will be suppressed. The thought of death having been suppressed, we become psychologically unequipped to face death when death confronts us.

REUVEN P. BULKA

The secularized 20th century technology as a creeping philosophy exacerbates the problem. Our cold and calculated sophistication,designed to mediate between humanity and nature in a this-wordly setting, almost ignores what may be called "the ultimate problems of being." The concerns of a dubious tomorrow are muted in the obsessive preoccupation with today. And, as long as death and what follows death are relegated to the "tomorrow," we, as part of the "today" world, will find it increasingly difficult to properly understand death.

To deal with the problem on a meta-clinical level we need an acceptable philosophy of life which fuses together the today and tomorrow, a philosophy which goes beyond the "as if" of a Camus, but is still more liveable than the *sein-zum-tode* of a Heidegger. If the today and tomorrow can be shown to be intermingled and intertwined, then perhaps the philosophical problems of death can be tackled. Then the resolution of the psychological component could follow.

In attempting to formulate a philosophy of life and death, we present two traditions, one religious, the other secular, relating to the role of death in life. The religious tradition is that found in the Talmudic and Midrashic literature of Judaism. The secular tradition is the logotherapy of Viktor E. Frankl.

TALMUDIC TRADITION

Even a cursory glance at the legislative structure of Judaism indicates a heightened appreciation for life. In Judaism, at all times, one is excused from the performance of a commandment when this endangers life (Talmud, *Yoma*, 85b). Danger to life suspends the affirmative code of Jewish existence. According to some (Maimonides, Mishnah Torah, *Laws of The Foundations of Torah*,5:4), this does not even allow one the possibility of being a theological hero. One *must* suspend religious observance for the higher reality, life itself.

Yet, the attitude to death in Judaism is surprisingly positive. Midrashic comment on the verse, "And God saw everything that God had made, and behold, it was very good (*Genesis*, 1:31), suggest that "very good" can be equated with death (Midrash Rabbah, *Genesis*, 9:5). In a similar vein, it is said of the psalmist

David that "He looked upon the day of death and broke into song" (Talmud, *Berakhot*, 10a).

We are thus confronted with an affirmative attitude to life and a positive outlook to death. In simple terms, the two ideas can be reconciled with the mediating principle that we would not be faced with the imperative "to act and accomplish" if life were endless. That existence may be terminated suddenly is a reality which forces, or should force, us to utilize the allotted moments as meaningfully as possible.

It seems, though, that passive awareness of death in the abstract is not deemed as sufficient for influencing one's behaviour. Thus, to prevent transgression, the Talmud proposes that one be mindful of where one is eventually going, to a place of dust, worms, and maggots (Talmud, *Avot*, 3:1). It is said of the righteous that they "set their death in the forefront of their thoughts" (Midrash Rabbah, *Ecclesiastes*, 7:9). And, a famous sage, in order to bring home the importance of awareness of death, suggested to his disciples that they repent one day before their death. He was immediately confronted with the expected question, "does then one know on what day one will die?," to which the sage responded, "Then all the more reason that one repent today, lest one die tomorrow, and thus one's entire life is spent in repentance" (Talmud, *Shabbat*, 152a). Repentance here is presented in the existential sense, as the constant process of investigating the past to improve the future.

We have here an ancient thought system which correlates the fact of death with meaningful life. There is a danger in proposing the view that one must be constantly mindful of death, as this can easily lead to neurotic behaviour. It is more realistic to take this extreme as a counter to the other extreme of neglect. The individual, in his/her own unique situation, must strike a delicate balance. This balance might rest in the awareness of death when one establishes the "game-plan" for life and in investing one's life energies in carrying out the plan.

The paradoxical nature of one's relation to death is best expressed in a dialogue between Alexander of Macedon and the elders of the south city.

He said to them: What shall a person do to live? They replied: The person should mortify the self. What shall a person do to kill the self? They replied: The person should keep the self alive. (Talmud, Tamid, 32a)

A Midrashic counterpart of the same idea is the following: "Death is near to you and far from you, as well as far from you and near you" (Midrash Rabbah, *Ecclesiastes*, 8:17). The more one is interested merely in keeping the self alive, the more one cuts the self off from meaningful living. In the pursuit of years one wastes the days. The more one realizes one is mortal, destined to die, the more one will try to accomplish, thus perhaps even gaining immortality. Basic to the Talmudic approach is the notion that death, properly understood, can be a vital life force.

The element of fear can easily enter into the religious sphere, as when one is urged to behave in a certain manner in life because of the consequences one might face afterwards. Such a confrontation with life and death out of fear, which might yield positive results on a quantitative level, nevertheless falls short on the qualitative level. To propose transcending death in an atmosphere of fear is to circumvent the trauma of death with an even greater disease, the life lived in fear. An affirmation of the role of death in life on an existential level would thus seem to be most appropriate. For this, we turn to the existential philosophy underlying the logotherapeutic system of Viktor E. Frankl.

LOGOTHERAPEUTIC THOUGHT

Logotherapy is the school of psychotherapy fathered by Frankl and focusing on the importance of meaning in life. It proposes the existence of unconditional meaningfulness and posits the view that the primary motivational force for humans is to find a meaning in life (Frankl, 1963, p. 154). Logotherapy, unlike other existential systems, is basically optimistic, future-oriented, and focuses on human freedom and the multitude of possitilities for individuals to find meaning. It carefully avoids injecting such ideas as fear, trembling, sickness-unto-death, nausea, anxiety, etc., into the human situation. Instead, ideas such as hope, meaning, joy, ecstacy, and values form its basic lexicon. Nevertheless, logotherapy does not recoil from facing squarely the issues of suffering and death.

The process of death, according to Frankl, is not a severed fragment of the human biography. Death is part of life. "Without suffering and death human life cannot be complete" (*ibid.*, p. 106). In projecting the notion of "unconditional meaningfulness," one is called upon to elicit meaning up to and including the moment of death. For "human life, under any circumstances, never ceases to have meaning, and this infinite meaning of life includes suffering and dying, privation and death" (*ibid.*, pp. 131-132). The thesis of logotherapy is that one is to live, and die, meaningfully.

So much for the moment of death. What bearing does the inescapability of death have on life itself?

Frankl believes the fact of death is crucial to life; "only in the face of death is it meaningful to act" (Frankl, 1968, p. 30). Contrary to the thought that death projects the futility and meaninglessness of life, Frankl asserts that if one's life tenure were really infinite in duration, one could continually, and legitimately, postpone every action forever. It would not really matter whether a deed was performed now, or ten years from now. "But in the face of death as absolute finis to our future and boundary to our possibilities, we are under the imperative of utilizing our lifetimes to the utmost, not letting the singular opportunities — whose `finite' sum constitutes the whole of life — pass by unused" (Frankl, 1968, p. 52).

The human exists in time and time exists in the human. In the becoming process, the person-time combination is utilized. The death of the human in time signifies the passing of a life. The death of time in the human signifies the passing of a moment. Ultimate death is only a more radical form of expiration, more radical than the death in installments involved in the wasting of time.

Proper utilization of time, on the other hand, signifies a positive irreversability, for that which has been accomplished remains as a reality forever. Transitoriness applies only to the potentialities, which, once actualized, are, so to say, "rescued...into the past" (Frankl, 1968, p. 30). Death poses a constant imperative to humanity, an imperative which says that each moment is irrepeatable, as is life itself, and must be utilized. Death makes life meaningful. The challenge of life is how to use each moment, which values are to be actualized, and which doomed to non-existence (Frankl, 1973, p. 191).

In logotherapy, this is taken to indicate the importance of the past, that "man's past is his true future" (Frankl, 1966, p. 365). The past deeds are "safely stored," immune from any erasure. And, for the dying person who has no future, the past, which is really one's life, is the eloquent testimonial to one's existence. Death ends the becoming process. In death the person "is." And the person "is" what the person was in life (*ibid*).

In order to counter the negativism usually linked to the fact of death, Frankl actually introduces the ubiquity of death even in life, in the passing of time, as a counter to nihilism. The fact that not only life, but also the moment, can be lost and are, in fact, irreversible, leads to the logotherapeutic notion of one's responsibleness in life. For, if what has been done can forever be undone, and vice-versa, then virtue and vice would disappear in uncertainty; praise and blame would be impossible and education unmanageable. Human beings would be free from the responsibilities which underlie their humanness. Responsibleness is a responsiveness to the challenges posed by life, challenges which call for undelayed response.

If the existence of the person in time is "temporality" and the existence of time in the person is "singularity," the following statement encapsules these ideas; "The meaning of human existence is based upon its irreversible quality. An individual's responsibility in life must therefore be understood in terms of temporality and singularity" (Frankl, 1967, p. 52).

Irretrievability of a past moment, singularity, and of a past life, temporality, constitute the basis of human existence and are the impetus for one's responsibleness to life. Frankl thus sees death as an ongoing life process, not in the pessimistic sense, but in the positive sense. Just as total death, the death of the person in time, challenges one's life in its totality, so fragmentary death, the death of time in the person, challenges the individual in each moment. The sum of these moments consitutes human existence.

COMMON AFFIRMATIONS

It is instructive at this point to note the striking similarities between the Talmudic and logotherapeutic attitudes to death. Although they are separate systems, the one religious, the other secular, nevertheless both take an affirmative attitude to death. The affirmative attitudes are no doubt born of differing assumptions. At work in the Talmud is the fundamental faith that God would not have put in the world a purely negative reality or fact of life. This is not to glorify or seek death, rather to indicate that death enhances the human situation.

In logotherapy one senses an optimism with life which is, at once, a philosophical and psychological proposition. As death is unavoidable, it is psychologically inappropriate and philosophically untenable to deny its importance. To avoid the dangers of negativism, which can only impede the human situation, it is vital to say yes to life in its totality. Even if life appears senseless, and death more than meaningless, it is vital for us to make life and death as meaningful as possible, to make life philosophically justifiable and psychologically liveable. In both these systems, there is an inherent affirmation of the natural order and an implicit faith in all life contingencies.

One may argue that logotherapy presents nothing new, that its ideas already appear centuries ago in the Talmud. Perhaps the uniqueness of the logotherapeutic approach is that it is so affirming while being a secular system.

For the person-in-the-street, however, theological or logical propositions are not likely to evoke any excitement. Theology and philosophy have a habit of finding the ear of few people. If Hegel is correct in saying history is what one does with death, then the 20th century poses a unique challenge. Some see in the proliferating abundance of life-saving techniques and their use on the dying person a denial of the individual's right to his or her own death (Kubler-Ross, 1970, pp. 8-9). It appears as if science is doing its utmost to see if it can beat the death force, if it can conquer nature. And ironically, the same medical prowess which tries to conquer death is the judge of when medicine can no longer help, when the

19

situation is hopeless to the point that euthanasia is indicated. In these attitudes one senses a trend to deny nature, to let medicine prolong, and, if need be, to terminate. The affirmative view of logotherapy is consistent when it asks if "we are ever entitled to deprive an incurably ill patient of the chance to `die his death,' the chance to fill his existence with meaning down to its last moment..." (Frankl, 1967, p. 37). For, "The way he dies, insofar as it is really his death, is an integral part of his life, it rounds that life out to a meaningful totality" (*ibid*, p. 37).

Perhaps what we should be arguing for is a return to nature, to an awareness and appreciation of the natural, unavoidable aspects of human existence. Fiefel hints at this when he argues that "the concept of death must be integrated into the self to subdue estrangement from the fundamental nature of our being" (Feifel, in Ruitenbeek, 1969, p. 129). Frankl alludes to it when he asserts that "this acceptance of finiteness is the precondition to mental health and human progress, while the inability to accept it is characteristic of the neurotic personality" (Frankl, 1968, p. 47).

In the striving for an orderly, structured world, a world of rules and clear-cut patterns which are undoubtedly necessary for technology to benefit the masses, how we relate to death has suffered from attempts to avoid the inevitable. We cannot confront death properly, we often do not grieve properly, and subsequently we do not live properly.

The ultimate answers relative to the problem are not logical but paradoxical. From the Talmudic dialogue previously cited that to live one must mortify oneself and to die one should indulge in life, to the Heideggerian idea that one can conquer death by actually willing it, to the logotherapeutic notion that the extent to which one understands one's finiteness, to that extent one also overcomes it (*ibid*, p. 36), it is evident that we magnify the problems of death by avoidance and counter these problems by accepting and affirming the role of death in life. In espousing an affirmative attitude to the natural order, it might be possible not only to effectively overcome the trauma associated with death, but also to re-enter into meaningful dialogue with life, and to project human concerns onto the forefront of our endeavours.

CHAPTER 2

RABBINIC ATTITUDES TO SUICIDE

It was Albert Camus who placed the matter of suicide in the most prominent place on the human agenda. He contended that "there is but one truly serious problem, and that is...judging whether life is or is not worth living" (Camus, 1955, p. 3).

Viktor Frankl, the father of the third Viennese school of psychotherapy known as *Logotherapy*, reports that a high school teacher once invited his students to submit to him, anonymously, any questions they might wish. The questions submitted were wide-ranging, including matters relating to sex, drug addiction, and life on other planets, "but the most frequent subject — one wouldn't believe it! — was suicide" (Frankl, 1978, p. 24). For Frankl, the question of the meaning of life, the unheard cry for meaning, is the crucial issue of contemporary life.

Suicide is not only the concern of many; it may also be more pervasive than we are led to believe. Pedestrian and auto accidents, excessive drinking followed by a self-destructive act, and other types of "accidental" deaths may be suicidal expressions. But,

> Religious and bureaucratic prejudices, family sensitivity, the vagaries and differences in the proceedings of coroners' courts and post-mortem examinations, the shadowy distinctions between suicides and accidents — in short, personal,

official and traditional unwillingness to recognize the act for what it is — all help to pervert and diminish our knowledge of the extent to which suicide pervades society. (Alvarez, 1974, p. 106)

THEORIES

Given that suicide may be more common than is currently accepted, it is interesting to discern what attitude the human sciences take toward suicide. Thio (1978) sees the theories of suicide as falling into two categories — the psychiatric and the sociological. In general, the psychiatric theories assume there is something wrong with the individual who commits suicide, while the sociological theories locate the crux of the suicide problem within the social structure. The theories of Freud and Durkheim are prime examples of the two trends of thought concerning suicide. Though they may be poles apart, these theories share one important notion. "Both see the individual's actions as the result of powerful forces over which he has only limited control" (Stengel, 1971, p. 56).

Apart from these approaches, there are those who see suicide as not necessarily a pathological act. Suicide may be committed by logically thinking people. This *balance suicide* follows "a rational evaluation of the pros and cons of further life" (Meerloo, 1968, p. 29). Such suicides indulge in radical accounting. If the cons outweigh the pros, then life is a failure and is to be terminated.

Alvarez points out that:

a serious suicide is an act of choice, the terms of which are entirely those of this world; a man dies by his own hand because he thinks the life he has not worth living (1974, p. 74).

Today, the public attitude to suicide, as Stengel points out, is less dogmatic than it was in the past (1971). Thio states that anti-suicide laws today are rare; where they do exist they are seldom enforced. It is useful to keep this tendency in mind when analyzing the Jewish attitude to suicide. Thio further claims that today

24

the post-suicide reaction is more likely to be a feeling of love for the self-killer, even if the person was not that well-liked in life (1978).

Perhaps the attitudes of human science and the general public are not unrelated. Alvarez claims that "modern suicide has been removed from the vulnerable, volatile world of human beings and hidden safely away in the isolation wards of science" (1974, p. 93). Approaching suicide as an unfortunate accident of social or psychic forces, as the case and theory may be, serves to excuse or even pity the suicide. This evokes feelings of love for the victim of circumstance.

Alvarez himself, peculiarly enough, seems to question the labelling of suicide, by sociologists and psychologists, as disease-related, as much as religions label it the most deadly of mortal sins. Alvarez thinks suicide is:

as much beyond social or psychic prophylaxis as it is beyond morality, a terrible but utterly natural reaction to the strained, narrow, unnatural necessities we sometimes create for ourselves. (1974, p. 307)

Alvarez himself is perhaps most indicative of how far con-temporary thought has moved relative to the suicide question. His views may not reflect the consensus, but they emanate from a more understanding, sympathetic stance.

SUICIDE AND JEWISH LAW

It is generally assumed that the so-called Judeo-Christian heritage takes a radically negative view of suicide (Farrar, 1951). There is a great danger in over-generalizing, whether it be in assuming an entity such as the Judeo-Christian heritage (Cohen, 1971), or in imputing to Judaism a one-sided, imbalanced attitude. Indiscriminately lumping together traditions detracts from and distorts the essence of these traditions.

On the statistical level, Jews have a lower suicide rate than Catholics and Protestants. But this can be misleading. For example, in the Netherlands, between 1900 and 1910, the Jewish suicide rate far exceeded the Catholic and Protestant rate. It appears that not only the type of religion but also the degree of religious liberalism affects the rate, with religious liberalism perhaps a more important factor (Thio, 1978).

Liberalism may sometimes express a lenient attitude within the tradition, but it is often indicative of a break away from tradition.

It is instructive to explore the Judaic attitude to suicide by examining the views of Jewish tradition as expressed in the major works of Jewish law.

The traditional Jewish attitude to suicide begins with a wholesale condemnation of the act. "One who destroys oneself wittingly has no share in the world-to-come" is a popular Jewish saying. Interestingly enough, Greenwald (1965) as well as many others, point out that there is no Talmudic or Midrashic source for this adage. It is simply a folk-saying. The fact that the folk adopted such a saying undoubtedly had its roots in the tradition itself. The saying is expressive of a negative attitude to suicide.

The suicide is considered guilty of murder, albeit non-prosecutable murder, as killer and victim are the same. Life is seen as a gift from God entrusted to the person, who may not exercise the rights of ownership — to destroy, but must exercise the responsibilities of trusteeship. The Talmud (*Baba Kamma*, 91b) interprets the scriptural words, "And surely your blood of your lives will I require," (*Genesis*, 9:5) as applying to one who sheds blood by one's own hands. Both the derivation and the law are codified by Maimonides (Mishnah Torah, *Laws of the Murderer and Guarding One's Body*, 2:3).

The suicide, in some respects, is considered even worse than the homicide. The suicide leaves no room for repentance from the act. Second, death, as a sentence from a legal tribunal, serves as a catalyst for Divine forgiveness. But the suicide has foreclosed this possibility. The suicide is also seen as radically rejecting the foundations of the faith (Tukacinsky, 1960).

Within this perspective, the suicide is more than merely "equated with murder" (Alvarez, 1974, p. 68).

Included in the category of suicide are actions which lead to a person's death through negligence, such as inciting a fight which leads to being killed, or walking a dangerous path, for instance, over ice in the winter and then falling into the water (Judah the Pious, 1970, para. 675). These actions are suicidal in outcome if not in intent. The broadened scope of suicide to include such actions is even more far-reaching than Stengel's insistence on defining the suicidal act as *"any deliberate act of self-damage which the person committing the act could not be sure to survive"* (1971, pp. 82-83). Stengel only goes so far as including deliberate acts of self-damage, whereas the Judaic view would include even negligence. One must answer for negligence, since in negligence one has failed to maintain watchfulness over life, thereby failing to affirm the sanctity of life. The religious perspective extends further than scientific categorization.

In fact, the Rabbis have forbidden many things because of their potential danger to life. Failure to adhere to these prohibitions make one liable to the punishment of "flogging for rebelling" (Maimonides, Mishnah Torah, *Laws of the Murderer and Guarding One's Body*, 11:5). The Rabbis, it may be said, tried to prevent even the passive suicide.

RIGHTS OF THE SUICIDE

The suicide is denied the normal rites of burial.

We do not occupy ourselves in any respect with the funeral rites of one who committed suicide willfully....We do not rend garments for him, bare the shoulder, or deliver a memorial address over him. We do, however, stand in a row for him and recite the benediction of mourners for him, from respect of the living (relatives). The general rule is: With anything that makes for respect of the living we occupy ourselves, but with anything that does not make for the respect of the living, the public does not in any way occupy itself. (Talmud, *Semahot*, 2:1)

The suicide is disconnected from the burial ceremony. Attention is focused on attending to the needs of the surviving family. No disrespect is hurled the way of the suicide, in deference

27

to the living, and any respect shown the suicide is for the sake of the living.

What is said at the burial of a suicide? Concerning this there is a difference of opinion. The view of Rabbe Yishmael is that we exclaim over the suicide, "Alas for a lost (life!) Alas for a (lost) life!" Rabbe Akiva disagrees. He says that we should leave the suicide unmourned. ~Speak neither well nor ill of him" (Talmud, *Semahot*, 2:1). Rabbe Yishmael speaks to the matter of consistency. If suicide is condemned in the tradition, it should then be lamented at burial, in order to affirm tradition and to hopefully prevent recurrences. Rabbe Akiva opines that silence is the best approach, either out of deference to the surviving family or out of consideration for the suicide. Perhaps there were extenuating circumstances which make blame inappropriate.

Within this difference of opinion between Rabbis Yishmael and Akiva, one finds the roots of the developing, and indeed complex, Judaic attitude to suicide; one which incorporates, at once, condemnation and understanding.

The precise term employed by the Talmud and later authorities to describe suicide is "destroying oneself wittingly" (*Me'abed atzmo lada'at*). This terminology relates to two aspects of suicide, the act (destroying) and the intent (wittingly). This would exclude the legitimate martyr, who is affirming rather than destroying life, as well as one who is not fully in control of his/her wits at the time of suicide. The martyr will be discussed later. Here attention is focused on the conditions which pertain to the aspect of "unwittingly."

INTENT AND SUICIDE

The basic rule of suicide is expressed in the Talmud:

Who [comes within the category of] "one who committed suicide willfully?" He does not who climbed to the top of a tree and fell down and died, or he who went up to the top of the roof and fell down and died. But he who calls out, "Look, I am going to the top of the roof or to the top of the tree, and I will throw myself down that I may die" [comes within the category]. When the people saw him go up to the top of a tree

28

or roof [for the purpose] and he fell down and died, he is presumed to have committed suicide willfully. (Talmud, *Semahot*, 2:2)

To satisfy the conditions for suicide, one must announce the intent for suicide and then carry out that expressed intention in the view of others. An intervening period of substantial duration between the expression and the act again disqualifies the act as suicide.

As in the Jewish law regarding capital crimes, with suicide there is a presumption of innocence.:

If a person was found strangled or hanging from a tree or lying dead on a sword, he is presumed not to have committed suicide wilfully, and none [of the rites] are withheld from him. (Talmud, *Semahot*, 2:3)

A more contemporary authority applies this ruling even to a case in which it is evident that the act was perpetrated by the victim, where homicide is ruled out. It may be self-killing, but it is assumed to be without one's full wits; the victim was overcome by an evil spirit (insanity?) or fear-evoking circumstance (Sofer, Yore Deah, Responsa 326).

Tukacinsky (1960) spells out the conditions which must prevail for an individual to be condemned as a suicide, to be denied the rites of religious burial. Even if a person announces the intention to shoot the self and is later found shot, the announced intention is not connected to the act. We assume that people talk in exaggeration and do not always mean what they say. Only if the victim connected the intention with the action is such a case eligible for the suicide label. Even if one left a note, it cannot be assumed that there is a direct connection between the suicide note and the act.

Tukacinsky further quotes authorities who rule out certain forms of self-killing as suicide. Even a drowning which follows immediately upon an expressed intention cannot be considered suicide. It takes a while for one to drown, time in which one wrestles with the agony of dying. It is assumed that in the few moments prior to death one repented from the act of self-killing (1960, p. 272).

Such exemption applies to any form of suicide in which there is an intervening period of consciousness between the act and death.

This liberal attitude is not inconsistent with the previously mentioned prohibition against any form of self-damage. One can maintain, at one and the same time, that every individual is *answerable* for the inflicting of damage on the self, but that not every self-inflicted death qualifies as suicide, with all the attendant restrictions imposed on the suicide. Answerability is an other-worldly concept, in God's hands. Suicide is a this-worldly judgement, made by people about others' actions.

> The law of destroying oneself is only conceivable in a situation where the victim himself established with absolute certainty that he killed himself with a clear mind, and without an intervening period for regret. (Tukacinsky, 1960, p. 272; translation mine)

Clear intent and a guarantee that this intent was never compromised are requisites for labelling an act as suicide. Tukacinsky cites a view that any individual who kills the self because of a multitude of troubles and worries is not considered a suicide. This would be a very liberal explication of the term "clear mind," and rules out the worried person from having killed the self "wittingly."

There are some who add another proviso to legitimize the suicide label. The suicide must have previously been forewarned by two witnesses that the act is criminal, of capital import, and the suicide accepted the warning. This is a precaution which is applied in most cases of capital crimes. Tukacinsky mentions the sources for this view and considers it strong enough to be relied upon when there is other supporting evidence mitigating the circumstances.

Forewarning is another way of establishing that the suicide was full witted when committing the act. The witnesses who forewarn must testify that the killer-victim was of a clear enough mind to absorb the message in sane receptivity.

Thus, though Judaism radically condemns the act of suicide, radical condemnation of the person involved is not so readily forthcoming. In the view of Rabbi Y.M. Epstein, we look for the slightest contingency to avoid branding an individual as a suicide (Arukh haShulhan, Yore Deah, 345:5).

Tukacinsky himself agrees with this view and adopts this stance as normative, but he rejects the view which would exclude one overcome by troubles and worries from being considered a suicide. If that were the case, says Tukacinsky, "there would be no instance of destroying oneself, because anyone who destroys the self does so because of pain" (1960, p. 273).

Tukacinsky would like the theoretical stance toward suicide to have some basis in fact. If there is no factual suicide possible, then there is no concept of suicide which is rooted in reality. Greenwald points out, however, that the sages searched so many times "for excuses and positive points about the one who destroyed the self wittingly, until there is not to be found, in truth, a case of one who destroyed the self wittingly" (1965, p. 319).

One can readily appreciate the danger in simply saying that Judaism radically condemns suicide. This fails to take into account the humane stance toward the killer-victim and the hesitancy to even employ the label of suicide, or to apply the legal fiat associated with suicide.

This approach, however humane and psychologically perceptive as it is, still remains seemingly inconsistent. The consistency of approach will be examined after further discussion of other exemptions from the suicide label.

OTHER EXEMPTIONS

The strict interpretation of "wittingly" serves to exclude other situations from consideration as suicide:

It is related of the son of Gorgias of Lydda that he ran away from school and his father pointed to his ear. In fear of his father he went and destroyed himself in a pit. They went and inquired of R. Tarfon who ruled: We do not withhold anything from him. (Talmud, *Semahot*, 2:4)

The Talmud gives another case of a minor who killed himself where the judgement was the same. The minor is by definition eliminated from consideration as a suicide; "a minor who destroys the self with full wits is considered as without full wits" (Shulhan Arukh, Yore Deah, 345:3).

A *shoteh*, one who is behaviourally deficient in one form or another, cannot be considered a suicide. The precise definition of *shoteh* as used in the Talmud is elusive, but it surely involves a condition which does not satisfy the "wittingly" principle.

A drunk, who has reached a state of inebriation in which sane behaviour does not prevail, is considered the same as a *shoteh*. The precise legal definition is here likewise elusive, but, as in the case of *shoteh*, as pertains to suicide, one is always given the benefit of the doubt.

Greenwald likewise lists, in the exemptions from suicide, one who kills oneself out of fear for difficult tribulations which will be hard to withstand; or because one feels one has sinned and is deserving of death, such that the act of killing is conceived as a penitence gesture.

The Talmud relates that on the day Rabbe died a Heavenly Voice (*bat kol*) announced that anyone who was present at the funeral of Rabbe was destined to share in the world-to-come.

A certain fuller, who used to come to him every day, failed to call on that day; and, as soon as he heard this, went up upon a roof, fell down to the ground and died. A *bat kol* came forth and announced: That fuller also is destined to enjoy the life of the world to come. (Talmud, *Ketuvot*, 103b)

A superficial reading of this incident inclines to the idea that the fuller acted out of frustration and depression, having missed just the very day which would have guaranteed him eternal life. A Talmudic commentary adds another dimension to the incident. Apparently Rabbe died on the eve of Shabbat. The massive outpouring of people attending his funeral caused the final rites to last late into the day. Afterwards people rushed home in order to make adequate preparations in time for Shabbat, but the multitude were anxiety ridden, in fear that they had, in fact, not made the

Shabbat deadline but had worked into the Shabbat. A *bat kol* from heaven, a Heavenly Voice, assuaged their anxieties by assuring all who were involved in the final respects to Rabbe of a share in the world-to-come; all except the fuller, according to the version in the Jerusalem Talmud. The fuller was excluded because he had not attended and had desecreted the Shabbat for reasons unrelated to Rabbe's funeral. In despair, and as an act of penitence, he jumped from the roof.

The biblical punishment for desecration of Shabbat is stoning, by which one is thrust down from a height and, if still alive, stoned. This is, in the main, a theoretical design as Jewish courts rarely meted out the death penalty. But this fuller acted as his own judge and jury, giving to himself the punishment he thought a court would give to him.

A *bat kol* then announced that the fuller too would share in the world-to-come (Shitah Mekubetzet, *Ketuvot*, 103b).

The Talmud tells of Rabbe Hiyya b. Abba, who was constantly wary of temptation. His wife dressed herself up as a town prostitute and attempted to entice him. She asked him to bring her a pomegranate from the highest bough, which Rabbe Hiyya did with dispatch. When he re-entered the house his wife was heating the oven. He jumped into the oven. His wife asked what was the meaning of this, and Rabbe Hiyya explained that he had been enticed and did not resist. His wife explained that it was really she, not the prostitute, but Rabbe Hiyya was not mollified; "my intention was evil" were his parting words (Talmud, *Kiddushin*, 81b).

The case of the fuller and the case of Rabbe Hiyya are both instances where the Talmud makes no comment about the act of self-killing. In the case of the fuller, he is even granted paradise. In both instances, were the individuals to ask a legal opinion — should they take their lives? — the answer would undoubtedly have been "No." There is an understanding silence for both these individuals.

The Talmud declares that it is forbidden to send a neighbour a barrel of wine with oil floating at its mouth. The reason is related to an incident:

It once happened that a man sent his friend a barrel of wine, and there was oil floating at the mouth of the barrel. He went and invited some guests to partake of it. When they came and he found that it was only wine he went and hanged himself. (Talmud, *Hullin*, 94a)

Again, we find no condemnation of the folly of suicide. Instead, it seems as if the sages adopt the attitude of condemning the circumstances leading to the suicide, even condemning and forbidding the action which here resulted in unnecessary death.

King Saul attempted suicide in order to save himself from the Philistines, whom he felt would debase him and eventually kill him. Jewish tradition exonerates his action (Midrash Rabbah, *Genesis*, 34:13), and the legal code specifically eliminates all Saul-type actions from being considered suicide (Shulhan Arukh, Yore Deah, 345:3). They are considered under coercive pressure and removed from the "normal" circumstance which must prevail to legitimize the act as suicide.

MARTYRDOM

Until now, attention has been focused on the "witting" aspect of killing oneself. The Talmudic term for suicide, it has already been noted, is "destroying oneself wittingly." The second element involved is implied in the term "destroying." The martyr does not destroy life; on the contrary, the martyr's sacrifice is viewed as affirming life. In the religious context, the martyr is seen as protecting the dignity of one's God-given soul.

Meerloo, in listing the various forms of suicide, speaks of altruistic suicide, which involves sacrifice to the code (Meerloo, 1968, p. 42). Frankl seems to have doubts about the validity of such suicide as a legitimate human expression:

It is certainly conceivable, theoretically, that suicide may sometimes be justified as a consciously offered sacrifice, that in such a case it may amount to a genuinely ethical act. We know empirically, however, that the motives of even such suicide arise in reality all too often from some resentment, or that at the end some other solution to the apparently hopeless situation would have turned up. We can, therefore, risk

34

the generalization that suicide is never ethically justified. (Frankl, 1967, pp. 40-41)

On an ethical level, Frankl's views strike a responsive chord with Jewish tradition. Ethical justification, however, does not extend to the religious domain, where a different set of principles apply. The theological judgements made concerning martyrdom must be seen in the context of the firm belief in afterlife. One who martyrs the self cuts the self off from the present, but not from the future.

One is obliged to martyr oneself when the alternative is idolatry, incest, or murder. In any other case, one must transgress the precept or prohibition rather than give up one's life (Talmud, *Sanhedrin*, 74a). There are other variables in this legislation, such as whether the situation is a private or public one, a royal decree or an individual action. In the case of a royal decree or a public scene, martyrdom is obligatory even for a minor precept. When one who is obliged to martyr the self fails to do so, it is considered a desecration of God's name, but the individual is not punished (Maimonides, Mishnah Torah, *Laws of the Foundations of the Torah*, 5:4). When one who is not obliged nevertheless martyrs the self, the view of Maimonides is that such an individual has committed a capital offense and will have to answer for the life needlessly given up (*Laws of the Foundations of the Torah*, 5:1). Others maintain that an individual has the legal latitude to be strict on the self and sacrifice life where religious dignity is involved (Shulhan Arukh, Yore Deah, 157:1).

The Talmud relates that when Rabban Gamliel was condemned to death, a Roman officer came to him offering to save him if Rabban Gamliel would guarantee the officer a share in the world-to-come. After this guarantee was given, the officer jumped off a roof and died. The Romans had a tradition that if one of their leaders died after a decree is made, the decree is nullified. Rabban Gamliel was thus saved by the heroic act of the Roman officer, for whom a Heavenly Voice declared that the officer is destined for the world-to-come (Talmud, *Taanit*, 29a). This was a martyr-type act which was certainly non-obligatory, but is lauded as an heroic, meritorious gesture. The officer knew that there was no way out for Rabban Gamliel save a sacrifice such as his own.

The maiden who killed herself to foil the designs of Herod and his pretensions to acceptability is an instance of martyrdom for the sake of dignity, of foiling the designs of those who would compromise life's sanctity. Had the girl lived, she would have been forced to live with Herod and thus give him credibility. As it is, the Talmud states that Herod preserved her body in honey for seven years, with one view even asserting that Herod had intercourse with her (Talmud, *Baba Batra*, 3b). This action of Herod serves to emphasize the validity of the girl's martyrdom.

The Talmud lauds those martyrs who gave up their lives to glorify the name of God (Talmud, *Baba Batra*, 10b; *Sanhedrin*, 110b). One such hero is Rabbe Akiva, who refused to buckle under to a Roman edict forbidding the practice and teaching of Judaism, and was executed by them. Rabbe Akiva could not visualize a meaningful Jewish existence without Torah; he compared this to a fish living out of water (Talmud, *Berakhot*, 61b). For him, the dangers of teaching Torah were not as severe as the consequences of living without Torah — the code of Jewish existence.

When they combed his flesh with iron combs, Rabbe Akiva was busy reciting the *Sh'ma* — the prayer for accepting upon oneself the yoke of the kingdom of Heaven. His students were astonished at this, but Rabbe Akiva exclaimed that he had been waiting so long to affirm his love of God even should God take away his soul. Rabbe Akiva yearned all his life to express his unconditional love for God (Talmud, *Berakhot*, 61b). For Rabbe Akiva, the martyr's death was an affirmation of life in its ultimate context.

A unique martyr situation is that which involved Rabbe Hanina ben Teradion. He too was sentenced to death for being occupied with Torah. He was surrounded by the Scroll of the Law, with branches around him, and then set on fire. To prolong the agony, tufts of wool soaked in water were placed on his heart to delay his passing. The executioner offered to intensify the flame and remove the wet tufts if guaranteed a share in the world-to-come. He did so after being thus guaranteed, and then jumped into the fire together with Rabbe Hanina. A Heavenly Voice then announced that both Rabbe Hanina ben Teradion and the executioner had been assigned to the world-to-come (Talmud, *Avodah Zarah*, 18a).

There are two aspects of this incident which merit comment. First, there was no real reason for the executioner to jump in save perhaps the fear that his superiors would punish him for his actions. The fact that he was able to take away the tufts of wool indicates that he may have been alone, for otherwise the other soldiers would have stopped him from exercising his human decency. Still, he was lauded by the Heavenly Voice. The executioner may have seen his self-killing as a means for ensuring his entry into paradise, on the shoulders of Rabbe Hanina.

Another interesting aspect of this incident is that Rabbe Hanina's disciples urged him to open his mouth so the fire could enter and kill him quickly, thus ending his agony. Rabbe Hanina replied, "Let Him who gave me [my soul] take it away, but no one should injure oneself" (Talmud, *Avodah Zarah*, 18a). Rabbe Hanina accepted the offer of the executioner to intensify the flame and remove the tufts; these were not his actions but those of the executioner. Also, they did not affect the inevitable. However, he refused by his own actions to accelerate death even by a few moments. In his martyrdom, Rabbe Hanina affirmed life and rejected a suicide which would have certainly been understandable.

Whilst Rabbe Hanina refused to inflict damage on himself, it is nevertheless considered permissible, even obligatory, to damage oneself, even to kill oneself, if one is unable to withstand the pressure to submit to the rejection of basic principles of faith. The Talmud relates in this vein that 400 boys and girls were carried off to be used for immoral purposes. Rather than submit to this outrage, they all threw themselves into the sea (Talmud, *Gittin*, 57b).

There are other instances of martyrdom, some of which are documented by Rosner (1970). For the purposes of this presentation, the instances cited herein are sufficient to illustrate how, within Jewish tradition, the negative attitude to suicide in theory is complemented by the view that under certain circumstances life is not worth living. These circumstances involve the compromise of principles so essential to life, such as immorality, murder, idolatry, and the absence of Torah.

REUVEN P. BULKA

BALANCED APPROACH

It remains as the final objective of this analysis to comprehend the logic of the Jewish attitude to suicide. If it is condemned in theory, why is suicide just about eliminated in fact?

The study of martyrdom showed that Judaism is concerned not only with quantity of life, but also with its quality. When a meaningful life is no longer possible, one surrenders oneself to one's Maker. But one must be sure that there is no other choice. Regarding self-killing when no martyrdom is involved, it is usually prompted by a situation in which the individual sees no future for the self. The suicide is not a leap into the afterlife; it is rather an escape from this world. Judaism cautions against this escapism: "And let not your [evil] inclination assure you that the grave is a place of refuge for you" (Talmud, *Avot*, 4:22). From the theological perspective, there is no escape.

The underlying common denominator in the Judaic attitude to suicide is the radical affirmation of the meaningfulness of life. Within this context there are two views, the prospective and the retrospective.

Prospectively, there is a confidence that life will afford the opportunity for fulfillment and that no situation legitimizes taking away what God has given. The Rabbis aimed at foreclosing the suicide possibility by condemning the act as legally forbidden and as morally and theologically reprehensible, consistent with Scriptural statements to that effect.

Retrospectively, for those who had already committed suicide, the Rabbis had much sympathy and understanding. In their affirmative stance toward life, they valiantly tried to see the affirmative in the suicidal act, or at least to see mitigating circumstances which would excuse the act as not being the *normal* expression of the killer-victim.

There is such a confidence about life that the Rabbis refused to believe that, in normal circumstances, one would take one's life. If that happened, it was obviously an abnormal expression, brought on by inner turmoil or external pressure (Cohn, 1976).

The Rabbis skate a thin edge, but by so doing incorporate theological doctrine and psychological insight, fusing into a humane, understanding approach.

The Rabbinic approach may be seen as the harbinger of the contemporary perceptions of suicide, although it remains dimensionally different and, in general, more farsighted.

CHAPTER 3

LONELINESS

Though the awareness that "it is not good for the individual to be lonely" (*Genesis*, 2:18) dates back to the Bible, the scientific study of loneliness is a relatively recent phenomenon, having come into the forefront mainly in the last decade. Robert Weiss, considered by many to be the primary guru of loneliness in North America today, mentions (1973) that research on loneliness was almost nonexistent until recently. The only clinician of note who actually paid much attention to it was Harry Stack Sullivan. He described loneliness as the exceedingly unpleasant and driving experience connected with the inadequate discharge of the need for human intimacy. It is a complicated way of saying that loneliness means being lonely!

LONELINESS AND SOLITUDE

What is loneliness? One must immediately differentiate between the experience of being lonely and the experience of being alone. The experience of loneliness has negative connotations to it, whereas the experience of being alone is perhaps best identified with "solitude." Solitude implies a condition which is not negative, but positive; a time for introspection, for self-investigation, for channeling one's resources in whatever way possible. There-fore, because of the negative impact of the term "loneliness" and the positive impact of the term "solitude," it would be useful to give some parameters of differentiation between the two terms. These are not exhaustive, but indicative of the difference between the two areas.

Loneliness does not usually come via choice. Solitude is chosen, it is desired. It is not imposed; rather, it is something natural to want. Josh Billings once said, "Solitude is a good place to visit, but a poor place to stay." But it is in our hands. Loneliness is not a desired state. In loneliness, one is aware of the condition - a state of being, which can sometimes lead to depression. In solitude, there is no excessive focus on the self, per se. Instead, there is a focus beyond the self, into the area of what one can do with one's self or with others. There is a more forward looking thrust to being in solitude than there is in loneliness.

Loneliness, to be sure, is not caused by being alone. It is caused by being without some definite needed relationship. Loneliness is more a feeling; aloneness, or solitude, is a state or a situation. Loneliness is simply exclusion when inclusion is de-sired.

The praise accorded to solitude leads one to think it is something to be sought out more actively. Thoreau is quoted as having said that he never found a companion that was so compan-ionable as solitude. Bruyere called it a great misfortune to be incapable of solitude, and Carl Sandburg, over a hundred years ago, said that one of the greatest necessities in America is to discover creative solitude.

Loneliness, we are beginning to find out, is a basic human condition. In a poll that was taken a little while ago, it was shown that within a period of any number of weeks, one quarter of all Americans avowed that they had been lonely during that period of time (Weiss, 1973, p. 1).

THE VULNERABLE

One of the interesting aspects related to loneliness is the question of who is more likely to be lonely, the young or the old.

INDIVIDUAL, FAMILY, COMMUNITY:
JUDEO -PSYCHOLOGICAL PERSPECTIVES

Weiss suggests that it is a sort of a curve that goes down in the middle, up in the younger ages, and up again in later ages. Yet others claim that the elderly are less lonely. This might seem a little bit surprising, but there are two varying theories as to why the elderly might be less lonely. One is the possiblity that they have already become acclimatized to loneliness since they have lived with it for a longer time and they are used to it by the time they reach that age. The other is that the effects of loneliness are premature death, leaving the scene of the world, so that those who have reached the age of 70 or 80 are the survivors who obviously were not lonely or overcame loneliness. This smacks of a Darwinian ethic, a survival of the fittest syndrome relative to loneliness (Rubin, 1979).

For adolescents, loneliness is most intense on Friday night and Saturday night, when everyone else is going out on dates, and there is a pressure to go out, but no one calls or there is nobody to call. Winter is usually the loneliest time of the year, except if one lives in the Caribbean, or some other sunny spot. The cold weather and its concomitant closed-in feeling breeds a low grade depression which derives from being detached from the world. But at the same time, human ingenuity is at work to escape from the constraints of winter. The sports of skiing and ski-dooing are ample testimony to this.

For those without a family, it seems as if those family situations which are of highest impact are the times which create the most loneliness, such as Thanksgiving, Passover, and the like. Where inclusion is desired, exclusion is felt most intensely. The media unconsciously conspires to convince the public that at certain times togetherness with family is as American as apple pie. For those with family, the media is a positive catalyst; for those who are alone, the media is a catalyst for despair.

People who are living alone are not more likely to say they are lonely than people who are living with others. In other words, both experientially and philosophically, it is not being alone that causes loneliness. Sometimes one can be amongst a significant number of people and still be lonely.

REUVEN P. BULKA

A BASIC CONDITION

Ernest Becker (1974) felt that loneliness is built into the basic human condition. Human beings who have a richer interior life are introspective by nature. Authentic loneliness emerges from the introspective look at the self. There is a dualistic tension between agape and eros, the tension between sameness and difference, the tension between wanting to be one of the crowd and also wanting to be a unique individual. This very tension leads to two types of loneliness. Agape fulfilled results in the loneliness of nonindividuation; eros fulfilled leads to the loneliness of separation from self.

This type of dialectical tension perhaps dictates that the human is programmed to a basic and intrinsic loneliness. This very tension may be at the root of the differentiation between different types of countries and different types of world views, between dictatorship and democracy; or, the polar anthitheses of sameness and uniqueness, the conformist model versus the uniqueness model. Ironically, Reisman claims that the lonely crowd of America is really an American society which is over-conformist by virtue of its inability to bear the loneliness of autonomy.

Since there is individual uniqueness or differentness, there is, therefore, loneliness. The sage Hillel once remarked, "If I am not for myself, who will be for me? If I am for myself only, what am I?" (Talmud, *Avot*, 1:19). These two statements deal with the very essence of the loneliness question. Basically, since each individual is unique, only the individual can understand his or her self. Hillel, therefore, asserts that no one will be able to put himself or herself into this position, to judge what he should be and where he should go. Hillel must be able to do this by himself. Hillel must be able to decide what his potentialities are, what the direction of his energies should be. However, Hillel says, if that solitude and that contemplation would result in his being for his self only, then he would be a deficient being.

One must begin with a quest within aloneness, within solitude, but that quest must reach outside one's own self. The famous, embracing rule —"Love your neighbour as yourself." (*Leviticus*, 19:18) — for which there are many homiletical interpretations, asserts that one must approach others with an appreciation of one's own self. If you do not like yourself, which means that when you are alone with yourself, you put yourself down rather than lift yourself up toward responsiveness, then you will approach others as a bankrupt personage. Loving your neighbour as yourself is founded on the assumption that in solitude, one must come to grips with and have a positive attitude towards one's own potentialities and capacities as a person.

It would be intriguing to contemplate the possibility of countering loneliness via computerized matching of diverse types, to fingerprint brainwaves and relate one individual's brainwaves to another. Is it possible, for example, to create some sort of physiological communion between two individuals? This was actually tried a little while ago in England, where one Dr. Gray developed what is called a toposcope and which was designed to connect individuals via brainwaves. In effect, Gray devised a system whereby the brainwaves given off by individuals show whether they are compatible or not. This would have been a scientific breakthrough in terms of countering loneliness. One could put brainwaves, almost like a fingerprint, into a computer system. The computer would then come out with a print of a matching brainwave and this would bring instant compatibility and togetherness. Loneliness would be banished forever.

Dr. Gray was a semi-heroic figure because he lived by his research. He found a girl who was compatible with his own brainwaves and married her in June. But the upshot of the story is that he divorced her in October on the grounds of incompatibility. Loneliness is a human condition which demands human reactions.

LONELINESS AND HELPLESSNESS

There is a powerful sense of loneliness or aloneness when one is unable to affect one's fate, when one is forced to deal with frustrations that may arise in so many ways. When one cannot make a contribution to affect one's own destiny, one feels forsaken, even alone in one's inability to climb out of the rut, especially when there is no one else to help. There is a feeling of isolation and detachment from the world. This can prevail in illness, in unem-

45

ployment, in tragedy. Instructive here are the basic Judaic norms which oblige the community of friends to visit the sick and the bereaved. This special obligation, in these instances, arises from the particular need for companionship, friendship, even attachment, when one feels detached from the vibrant world.

The norm of visiting the sick attempts to strike a delicate balance. Thus, Jewish law urges the visitor to be alert to the signals, to apprehend when the patient desires companionship and when the patient desires to be alone (Shulhan Arukh, Yore De'ah, 335).

Similarly, visiting the bereaved should begin with the third day of mourning. The initial period of mourning is in aloneness, even loneliness, but more a necessary solitude to confront reality in the privacy and protectedness of one's individual emotions (Talmud, *Moed Katanm* 27b). Having done this, the mourner is at least partially receptive to those who desire to assuage the grief.

All of these guidelines have a common denominator — the fact that one cannot extricate one's self from a helpless situation. Theologically, this is the essential problem of Job. Job is stripped of everything, his possessions, his family, his well-being. He cannot come to grips with this fate and is a helpless, forlorn, lonely figure. He has friends, but they effectively do little to lift him from his melancholy. Finally, when God speaks to him, Job is comforted. It is nothing God says, merely the fact that God is talking to him. Until then, Job felt rejected by God and thus lonely in an ultimate sense. God's talking to him was the ultimate reassurance that Job was not alone without God, which for Job was the most severe form of loneliness.

Mental health has been described as the capacity to balance relatedness to others with the ability to stand alone; not to be totally immersed in the self, as that can be dangerous, and not to be overly concerned about others to the point of neglect of the self, which is ridiculous. There must be a delicate balance.

Frieda Fromm-Reichman wrote in 1959 that loneliness, in its own right, plays a much more significant role in the dynamics of mental disturbance than we have so far been ready to acknowledge. Fromm-Reichman felt that the theories of loneliness were less than adequate because it had been studied so little. However, even now, scientific information concerning loneliness is hard to come by.

Weiss believes that part of the reason for this is that people tend to underestimate their encounters with loneliness. They have difficulty recalling later on the times that they were lonely. Those are the times they would like to forget, the times when they were "not themselves." Also, there is a strong possibility that loneliness is perceived by both professional and lay people as individual choice, a desired state which offers some form of perverse gratification, which beckons for and often receives the pity of others. This leads to a rejection of the lonely and under-attention to the problem of loneliness.

THE MODERN CONTEXT

Twentieth century North America, for various reasons, is a virtual breeding ground for loneliness. The nuclear family structure is a very closed-in institution, what Philippe Aries has termed a "prison of love." Children grow up in the nuclear family structure and, owing to the proliferating divorce rate, there are an increasing number of households which are not even nuclear. They are, rather, a single parent structure; the parent and child are forced to get along since there is no significant other in the household with whom to relate. However, there are always times of crisis, explosions of varying proportions which compromise the relationship between parent and child. The person whom the child looks to for affirmation of self is often the person who, in frustration or anger, berates the child. The child, therefore, grows up without an unswerving affirmer of the child's personhood.

The guilt feelings that children often have as a result of the evil wishes they harbour against their parents are not unrelated to the prison like structure into which they are locked.

Insightful observers, such as the late Margaret Mead, have argued that American society desperately needs community structures which allow for the interaction of generations, a set-up which would depressurize the parent/child relationship and bring back the omnipresent admirer of children who is always there with a pinch of the cheeks or a candy bar. With all the arguments, however, North America seems to be veering more and more towards increasing privatization, and what may aptly be called a human brand of single cell anemia.

When Brandeis asserted that "the right to be let alone is the most comprehensive of rights and the right most valued in civilized man," he may have been making a valid empirical observation. However, the effects of loneliness would indicate that the psychological validity of such a feeling is questionable. People value privacy, they have structured their lives around a specific degree of insular existence and do not wish to be bothered by the outside world. Granted that privacy can emanate from positive causes, such as the desire for solitude, or to be able to think and to recover one's physical and psychological equilibrium. At the same time, however, the penchant of many people for privacy is a euphemism for "I don't want anyone to bother me."

There does come a time in everyone's life when friends are needed and they cannot be magically created in the time of crisis. They must be nurtured through the good times.

The general feeling engendered by a social mass is one of alienation from the mass. Slater (1970) points out that Americans tend to see the people around them as nuisances. When everyone is rushing either to or from work or the stadium and the heavy traffic impedes one's progress towards a destination, everyone in front becomes, either consciously or sub-consciously, the enemy, the person or persons who are blocking the achievement of the goal.

Modern psychology knows of big city neurosis caused by being constantly surrounded by a frightening mass of people. The new science of proxemics, which may be a modern explication of the old Judaic notion of all individuals having their own "four amot" (4 cubits), as a basic territory (Talmud, *Baba Mezia*, 10a), deals with the space that a normal person needs away from the encumbrances of the mass in order to remain sane. Think of what happens when people enter an elevator. Chances are that anyone who enters an elevator will go to the corner that is furthest from another person or persons who are in the elevator, unless, of course, the person is an acquaintance. Those who are not acquaintances are strangers, even alien, part of that nasty mass that is always in the way.

Moustakas (1961) observes that modern industrial workers are separated from any direct and personal contact with creation. The assembly line worker repeats the same monotonous tasks daily, weekly, monthly, and yearly. There is no sense of achievement when all one does every day is to screw a few bolts into place at the right time. Volvo, in Sweden, has experimented with a different form of assembly line system, where workers rotate their specific tasks and, therefore, get a sense of what it is like to be involved with the whole. The loneliness that derives from work that has little coherence is merely the other side of the coin, that is, meaningful achievement brings a sense of fulfillment and even ecstasy.

Recent experimentations have shown that industrial accidents, which occur too frequently in assembly line jobs, occur to a lesser degree amongst workers who kiss their spouses before they go off to work. There is no magic in a kiss, but there is great benefit in knowing that you have someone worthwhile to come home to after the drudgery is done. Failing that, loneliness and detachment can easily become an "I don't care attitude," which leads to accidents. Every individual needs to have some sense of self-importance, a sense that one matters, that one counts. This need not come from work and it need not come specifically from the home; but it must come from somewhere. Unfortunately, North America seems to be choking all the sources.

Maslow long ago pointed to the therapeutic value of seeing a beautiful sunset or other wonder of nature (1971). This type of peak experience elicits a feeling which is the very opposite of loneliness — a mystical feeling of being at one with nature so that there is no question as to the meaningfulness of life and its beauty. There is nothing more beneficial to one who feels detached from the world, even totally insignificant, than to unite with it by experiencing one of the wonders of nature, no matter that the wonder is experienced alone.

It becomes more and more clear that loneliness is the hidden agenda in so many problems that have other labels. In the hyper-paced lifestyle that is characteristic or North America, even when one can form meaningful relationships, it is rare that this can be formed with more than one individual. Trust is often a matter of putting all of one's eggs in one basket. If it lasts, it may be ideal, but it may often become a case of excessive dependency or misappropriated trust. The devastation that results from being betrayed or disappointed by the one you trust has been aptly labelled by Harper "a psychological curse" (1974). In a society where having many friends is the exception rather than the rule, such psychological curses are likely to happen in greater abundance.

DIFFERENT MANIFESTATIONS

In general, Weiss suggests that people need two types of relationships — a sense of attachment and a sense of community. The sense of attachment usually comes from a spouse, the sense of community from a network of friends. Very acute loneliness would arise out of an absence of attachment. It is often the case that the absence of an attachment, or emotional isolation, leads to social isolation. Indeed, so much of a relationship is formed on a couple-to-couple basis, and when the couple aspect disintegrates, the basis of friendship goes with it. The remedy for these situations, quite logically, is the replacement of the missing provision. The prospect of replacement may forestall a budding loneliness.

Separation distress, for example, fades with time and becomes loneliness only when no new relationship is formed. Loneliness emanating from separation can arise even when the relationship was an unhappy one. Even the initiator of the divorce can be overcome with loneliness.

One salient manifestation of loneliness in America is evidenced in the canine syndrome. People today are tending towards smaller families and more dogs. Many psychological clinics would have fewer clients if the parents of the patients would treat their children with as much affection as they treat their dogs. Dogs are quite an effective counter to loneliness; they do not ask for increases in allowance, they do not ask for the keys to the car, they do not bicker about how you look, what you do or fail to do. They give unconditional affection. Many acquaintances have legitimized to me their having a dog because they dislike being greeted with more complaints and demands after a hard day's work. There is nothing that beats the feeling of knowing that whenever you arrive home, there will be a person (four legged) who will rush to shower you with affection. Instant gratification at its best!

With a dog, it is very difficult to feel lonely. Today, a dog is not only man's best friend — often a dog is man's only friend. The irony is that we often treat our family as dogs and our dogs as family. The dog, therefore, is North America's national monument to loneliness. It is self-evident that those who live alone and have dogs quite consciously do so to avoid the lonely feelings that may be caused by being alone.

There is another type of loneliness which has perhaps been most acutely felt by the Jewish people over the centuries, the loneliness of the group. Whether in security or in desolation, Israel is described as being alone — "And Israel dwells in safety, the fountain of Jacob alone..." (*Deuteronomy*, 33:28), or "O how the city that was once so populous remained lonely like a widow" (*Lamentations*, 1:1).

So much for Jewish observations of the Jewish condition. Balaam's perception was not that much different. He said of Israel — "It is a people that shall dwell alone and shall not be reckoned among the nations" (*Numbers*, 23:9). It appears as if the United Nations is doing its utmost to ensure the eternal validity of Balaam's prophecy. To be sure, Israel is not the only people that have suffered from group loneliness, but its loneliness has been a perpetual constant, especially over the last 2,000 years. In exile, they were lonely and vulnerable, often the victims of wanton and unchecked hatred. In the relative prosperity of the latter half of the 20th century, they are alone almost because they have overcome their vulnerability by becoming relative masters of their destiny. The loneliness of Israel as a group forged a sense of closeness within the group. Walking down a regular street, one may reflect on the thought of the differentness of everyone else, but when walking in friendly Jewish neighbourhoods one is often greeted even by strangers. Another Jew, however strange, is a companion survivor, part of the group.

The strength of the traditional Jewish home was certainly enhanced because it was an antidote to group loneliness. Of course, the traditional Jewish home of the past was a big home, a conglomerate of homes known as a shtetl. The North American penchant for privacy has affected the home today, so that there are very few shtetl-like Jewish communities remaining in North America.

Ritual expressions within Judaism remain a function of a religious imperative, but they have also gained greater viability over the ages as a concrete form of group expression, forging and solidifying a group feeling.

Today's political climate, ironically, places the United States in almost the same lonely position as Israel. The strength of family and community, so sorely lacking in North America, would do much to help the morale of the country.

While many people lament the economic downturn running its course in the Western world, there may be great benefit arising from this trend. People who cannot afford their own private homes may be "forced" into shared living arrangements. This may not be good for privacy, but it certainly goes a long way towards forging bigger and more cohesive communities and thus, in a larger sense, group and national solidarity.

CONSEQUENCES

The awareness of loneliness is both evident and useful in many situations. One of the more successful ways of overcoming overweight has been Weight Watchers. Alcohol problems have been effectively treated by Alcoholics Anonymous. In many cities, those who have experienced the misfortune of mastectomies, ileostomies, colostomies and the like have formed clubs comprised of people who have gone through the trauma. They share with each other, experience with each other and help those who are potential "newcomers" to the club. Underlining all these manifestations is that ubiquitous category - loneliness. While many have chosen a dog as their best friend, others choose the plate or the bottle. They are alone and lonely and try to either eat or drink away their misery. The effectiveness of a diet, or abstinence, is greatly enhanced by being kept within a group, the group being the counter to the loneliness which often is the malaise that gave birth to the syndrome. Those who have undergone any of the "...tomys" undoubtedly feel a sense of differentness. Clubs which unite the individual sufferers into a group serve to strip the sense of differentness which, in these instances, could easily erode into loneliness.

Loneliness is very often costly. Lynch (1977) points out that for similar illnesses, those over seventeen who are alone spend, on the average, thirteen and one-half days in the hospital, whereas those who are married spend, on the average, eight and one-half days (p. 209). One may interpret this more along functional lines; that is, one is likely to stay in hospital longer when there is no care available at home, simply because recovery is more difficult when one is alone. It may even be the physician's choice in many instances that those who are alone stay longer in hospital. Other statistics, however, seem to implicate loneliness. Those between 45 and 64, who are either widowed or divorced, visit doctors 5.9 times per year. Their married counterparts visit doctors only 4.6 times per year. This even though 78% of the married, 64% of the single, 59% of the divorced, 56% of the widowed, and 45% of the separated have hospital insurance, such insurance understandably militating in favour of more visits since there is less cost (ibid.).

A study of 10,000 Israeli adults who were monitored at random showed, in retrospect, that those with unsatisfactory marriages were more likely to become heart victims (p. 67). The classic formulation of Type A behaviour as a description of the personality type who works at a feverish pace is often a very lonely individual who overcompensates for the loneliness through the compulsion to produce, much like Kierkegaard. Kierkegaard produced, but he also died prematurely. Freedman and Rosenman of Type A fame have suggested, as an antidote for Type A personalities, that they become involved in human companionship, to attach to life, and therefore, to live.

Loneliness, it is becoming increasingly clear, can kill. The emotional deprivation syndrome known as marasmus is unique to the human species. Children who are denied love can die. In the animal kingdom, a newborn runs away from the mother into autonomy almost immediately after birth. The human child cannot do this either biologically nor psychologically. At the other end, dying alone combines the worst elements of an already bad situation. Kubler-Ross, for a long time, has suggested that terminal patients who are beyond medical salvation should return to their homes and be with their families rather than die surrounded by the antiseptic walls of an impersonal hospital. In California, an enterprising group created a new corporation called Threshold Inc. The service they offer is to provide companions to the dying. For a fee, they will supply a companion "till death do they part."

COMPANIONSHIP

We come back to the dog, which, insofar as loneliness research is concerned, may indeed prove to be one of man's best friends. Lynch reports experiments with dogs to which shocks were administered. Normally the administering of a shock would increase the dog's heart rate. However, if the dog was petted while being shocked, the heart rate increase was only half as great. In another experiment, if a dog was conditioned to a tone which was heard ten seconds before the shock, the heart rate increase was in the order of fifty to one hundred beats per minute just for hearing the tone. However, if the dog was petted continually, there was no heartbeat increase with the sound of the tone and surprisingly, there was no increase even through the administration of the shock (pp. 169-170).

Togetherness in pain is shown to alleviate significantly the symptomatology associated with the pain. Companionship may heal where loneliness would harm. Even a dog knows that!

It is difficult to estimate how many bad marriages have arisen because of a desire to escape loneliness. In many circles, being alone is a stigma and being single a curse. It starts very early, with the parental pressure to go out on weekends, and it may escalate into a tragic life.

It is very difficult to pinpoint the precise relationship between loneliness and depression, although it is generally felt that loneliness can often lead to despair and depression. From a depressed state, anything can happen, and it is usually unpleasant. Loneliness, then, is as potentially dangerous as it is ubiquitous.

The *Book of Proverbs* contains a multi-faceted testimony to the advantage of companionship. "Two are better than one, for they get better return for their labour." This relates to the pure physical aspects of togetherness, where two individuals working together are able to do much more and do it better. "For should they fall, one can raise the other, but woe to him who is alone when he falls and there is no one to raise him." This proverbial sentence reflects on intellectual loneliness. Two who think together can correct each other; they can be attuned to the oversights and mistakes of the other, to the overgeneralizations and oversimplifications; two can challenge and prod one another through intellectual exchange. One can make mistakes and be totally oblivious to them. As the Talmud asserts, "A sword on those who spend their entire lives studying alone" (*Berakhot*, 63b). Also, "If two sleep together they keep warm, but how can one be warm alone?" This statement deals with the need for emotional companionship, to immerse one's self in an other, to literally share life. Finally, "Where one can be overpowered, two can resist attack" (*Proverbs*, 4:9-12). This may be seen as a proverbial prophecy about life in the big cities! More realistically, it addresses the matter of survival capacity, which is enhanced through togetherness.

The work potential, intellectual abilities, emotional stability, and pure survival capacity of any individual are greatly improved by being together with someone else. This is the very stuff which brings out the best in human beings. The radical statement, "either companionship or death" (Talmud, *Taanit*, 23a), relates to the attrition of the human will to live that derives from lacking companionship.

Loneliness can lead to death even in a physiological sense. Lynch points out that the death rate is likely to be much higher in common illnesses for individuals who are alone, without any friends to care for them (pp. 40-43). The living death of depression is another outgrowth of companionlessness. Therapy, as we know it, is to a large extent an individual attempt to "buy for the self a friend" (Talmud, *Avot*, 1:6). For an hour a week, one buys an individual who will listen, commiserate, empathize, and perhaps even advise. If loneliness is at the root of the problem, then it really does not matter to what school the therapist is attached. The increasing evidence that neither the technique of the therapist nor the method of approach really makes that much difference is not that surprising.

Menninger, one of the leading therapists of this generation, once asserted that more is accomplished between two friends over a cup of coffee than hours of therapy. "If you have an anxiety within you, relate it to others" (Talmud, *Yoma*, 75a). Where there are no others, find a therapist. In most instances, others are better than therapists. They are natural friends rather than surrogates. They care deeply and are actively involved in helping. They are usually from the same social station rather than strangers from the upper crust who make caring a job.

CULTIVATING SOLITUDE

Having described the pervasiveness of loneliness, it is now apropos to seriously consider what can be done to counter loneliness.

The first step in countering loneliness involves cultivating a prudent attitude to solitude. It is vital to overcome the fear of solitude. For many, solitude is something to be avoided. It conjures up the frightening images of the terror of loneliness, but it need not be so. In the words of one observer, "Loneliness can hurt, but we have to admit that aloneness can heal" (Seudfeld, in *Rubin*, 1979). Hyperactivity, as well as high decibel experiences, are overcompensating stimulae to drown out loneliness. The toll that this exacts on a human being has already been discussed. Quiet, in its pristine sense, is a more effective antidote.

The parent whose child is"unfortunately" all alone for the weekend is better advised to encourage the child to use the free time for the self, rather than lamenting the loneliness. Lamenting the loneliness serves to make the child feel badly about being alone and thus feel badly about one's self. After all, if one is good, is it not nice to be in one's own company? At the same time, this also fosters a feeling of having been rejected. The negative self-image which is imposed upon the child can easily become a self-fulfilling prophecy.

INDIVIDUAL, FAMILY, COMMUNITY:
JUDEO -PSYCHOLOGICAL PERSPECTIVES

Cultivating solitude begins at a very early age. It is paradoxical, yet nevertheless true, that being able to manage and to
grow in aloneness is one of the better preventives of loneliness. In
aloneness and in solitude one can meditate, learn about one's self,
gain a solid footing in life, and thus be a much better partner for
others. Paradoxically, through being alone, one is more able to be
together.

East is east and west is west and never the twain shall meet.
But the west would be much better served if it gleaned from the
east the capacity to meditate, to relax and think. Such an aloneness
exercise is healthy for the body and healthy for the soul.

Edison once remarked that "the best thinking has been done
in solitude. The worst has been done in turmoil." Cultivating
solitude is a vital educational tool. Reading, research, intellectual
development are all greatly accelerated if one is able to properly
use time alone. Intellectual partners can do much, but what is
learned in solitude is the base from which all else emanates. Here,
too, one finds a delicate balance in Judaic prescription. One is
obliged to study, to meditate, to perfect one's self and at the very
same time, one is obliged to share one's knowledge with others.
Suppression of teaching is considered to be a grave sin (Talmud,
Sanhedrin, 91b). A healthy balance between learning and teaching
is thus a golden mean which incorporates solitude and companionship.

In North America, the fear of loneliness is most evident in the
famous cliche, "A family that prays together stays together."
Prayer has thus been escalated into a social experience. Much of
North American Jewish life has been affected by this slogan, a
catch-all phrase which reflects the fibre of church worship and
which has influenced many Jewish religious institutions. Saying
prayers may be a social experience, but actual praying is not.
Prayer is meditation; prayer is confrontation with one's self. In
prayer, one is alone with God and with one's self. According to the
Talmud (*Berakhot*, 32b), the original pietists would warm up for
prayer through one hour's preparation, then they would pray and
then take another hour to wind down, to go from the transcending
(and thus alone) experience of prayer into a spiritual decompres-
sion chamber.

REUVEN P. BULKA

To shake or not to shake — that is the question! One can stand stoically amongst a mass and read responsively, mouthing the words that have been programmed. While this has definite positive points, it is not the equivalent of the sobering and cleansing experience of *shaking* off the shackles of the world and leaping into the ecstasy of transcendence. Most people are afraid to unhitch and take a ride. In prayer, they do not let go, their feet are planted firmly on the ground and their bodies are as unmoving as the synagogue furniture. In escaping from the supposed terror of aloneness, which all too often is equated with loneliness, we have desacralized prayer into a social experience. A much better phrase would be — "A person who prays alone is well put together." Once again, this is not to reject the notion of public prayer, which is engrained in the Jewish heritage. It is rather to decry the lamentable pattern of escape from solitude, solitude being a vital ingredient even in public prayer.

The truly religious person has the advantage of feeling a link to God, a link which continually encourages and sustains. There is always "an eye that sees and an ear that hears" (Talmud, *Avot*, 2:1). The religious person is always driven and never lonely. The pseudo-religious person, who probably makes up a greater percentage of the Jewish population than we dare guess, is not so advantaged. The pseudo-religious person lives in constant expectation of good things from God and is likely, at the slightest adverse turn, to question God's right to inflict such adversity. The self-imposed detachment from God, which arises from this one-sided theology, can be a very lonely feeling, one which many Rabbis and counselors have been hard-pressed to correct.

The question of maintaining an open door policy has been one of the major national issues. It is also a local issue. It would be advantageous to follow an open house policy with special implications for the grandparent generation. After the holocaust many Jewish families were simply unable to have a trans-generational home. Now, however, this is more possible. Trans-generational interaction can be a tremendous boon to family functioning. It takes the pressures off parents since grandparents can do some of the disciplining (of course, they can hardly be expected to discipline when they see their grandchildren on rare occasions; then they are more likely to spoil). Parents need not demand respect and honour from their children; the children can pick it up just from the way their own parents behave towards the grandparents. Most importantly, grandparents are usually the best babysitters, readily available and always free.

While privacy is a need, it should not be all-encompassing, excluding other needs. With grandparents in the house, the occasional vacation can be a more meaningful experience in sharing than it being a continuing environment of perpetual privacy. The ebb and flow of contrasts in intensity of relatedness is a healthy variable in marriage. Within religious tradition, this ebb and flow is programmed into the marriage relationship via the laws of menstruation, which prescribe physical separateness for a designated period and then prescribe a physical renewal at the conclusion of that period. The couple have a period of time for themselves when they are guaranteed a certain modicum of privacy and solitude and, at the same time, they are guaranteed a companionship which is enhanced by the heightened expectations.

In families which do not adhere to these norms, one often finds a surrogate expression of this notion, such as when couples decide to cool it for a specific period of time, or to withdraw periodically. It may not be "good for the individual to be alone," but it is not healthy to be together too much. Balance involves oscillating between the two in a healthy pattern.

OUTER-DIRECTEDNESS

Not everyone treats loneliness with kid gloves. Gotz (1974) insists that if an individual is in the throes of a grieving mood emanating from loneliness, it is the choice of the person. Loneliness, he says, is bad faith, a narcissistic infatuation with the self. The focus on the self is, as far as Gotz is concerned, a basic ingredient of the lonlienss syndrome.

Self-expression comes in varying doses. In its extreme, it can irreversibly suppress the self which beckons to be expressed. However, it can also be expressed in more moderate doses. One can relate to others for the sake of fulfilling one's self; one can marry because it satisfies a need. There is no true relatedness in such a relationship. It is rather self-gratification which is, at times, mutual, and at other times one-sided. Self-gratification, or its more grandiose euphemism, self-realization, can claim much of the blame for the skyrocketing divorce rate in America. Weiss (1975) goes so far as to say that he knows of no divorce in which self-realization was not a factor in the break-up; if not the major factor, then at least a contributing factor (pp. 8-10).

Viktor Frankl's logotherapy is perhaps the most outstanding example of a therapeutic system which has grasped the importance of going beyond self-expression into the domain of self-transcendence, towards immersing one's self in either another cause or another person. The insular focus on the self, which is a characteristic of the lonely, is also characteristic of a deficient relationship or a deficient personality. The mature, well-oriented individual finds meaning and fulfillment via fulfilling others. When the focus of concern is the other, the concerned individual becomes the primary beneficiary. This is the manifestation of true love as opposed to mere infatuation (Frankl, 1967).

This is not to argue that individuals should be totally unconcerned about their own selves. If they are unconcerned about their own selves and even deride their selves, they cannot be effective partners. Hillel's balance is what is called for; intelligent concern for the self and devoted concern for the other.

Adler once advised a lady who complained of being depressed to spend the first half hour awake each day thinking about how she could bring joy to another and her depression would go away. A marital partnership in which each partner's major concern is to bring joy to the other is the ideal relationship. Evidence from the clinic has shown that an overwhelming percentage of sexual dysfunction is strongly linked to the narcissistic "what's in it for me?" syndrome. When the focus is on pleasing the partner, the gratifier is much more likely to become the gratified. This also translates into the day-to-day affairs of the house.

Such matters can sometimes be carried to an extreme. The Malagasy tribe, in its concern for the departed, remove the relatives from the grave once every three years after death and return them home for a visit so that they should not be lonely! We may recoil from the idea but should not recoil from the underlying ethos at work.

Two paradoxes are the salient features of any confrontation with loneliness. One is that in cultivating solitude and aloneness, we are able to counter loneliness; the other is that concern for others is the best vehicle for fulfiling one's self. Since loneliness is related to feeble attitudes to solitude and excessive concern with one's self, these paradoxes must become truisms if we are to win the struggle against loneliness.

CHAPTER 4

HONESTY vs. HYPOCRISY

The experiences of Judaism in America are subject to many interesting and often unpredictable fluctuations. Life as a Rabbi in a Jewish community is always a challenge, for it is hard to anticipate what novel situation may soon emerge, and what response to make to it.

A little while ago a young couple came by to bid me farewell before their vacation trip. In the course of conversation it developed that unfortunately but unavoidably, they would be flying on Shabbat. I seized this opportunity to suggest that they order kosher meals for the Shabbat flight. They laughed, thinking this was a facetious but insubstantial remark. However, I persisted, and, after a lengthy debate of the pros and cons, they concluded that they could not order the kosher meals, as that would be hypocritical.

The intellectual honesty of the couple is beyond question. What must be questioned is whether ordering kosher meals for a Shabbat flight is itself hypocritical. The larger question raised is that of consistency in observance as opposed to keeping some precepts and neglecting others.

In the existential climate of our times, which emphasizes the intimate link between inner feeling and outward expression, desecrating Shabbat and eating kosher at the same time is not characteristic of consistent behaviour. This chapter attempts to explore some Jewish sources relative to the problem and to understand the meaning of hypocrisy as it applies in the day-to-day encounter.

BASIC PARAMETERS

The dictionary definition of a hypocrite is a "person who pretends to have moral or religious beliefs, principles, etc., he does not actually possess." When we use the term hypocrite, it refers to one who purposely projects a false image of virtue. An unconcsious, but equally false image projection would not elicit a negative reaction of the same intensity.

. The Talmud addresses itself to the matter of hypocrisy in positive and prohibitive terms. On the positive side, the Talmud asserts — "Your `yes' should be just and your `no' should be just" (*Baba Mezia*, 49a). According to Abaye, this means that "one must not speak one thing with the mouth, another with the heart" (ibid.). In this concise statement the Talmud introduces the concept of integrity, wherein the outer expression and inner feeling are integrated with each other in honest communication.

There are some legal exceptions. One obvious exemption is in times of danger. Thus,

When Ulla went up to Israel he was joined by two inhabitants of Hozai, one of whom arose and slew the other. The murderer asked Ulla, "Did I do well?" "Yes," he replied. "Moreover, cut his throat clear across." When he came before Rabbe Yohanan, he asked him, "Maybe, God forbid, I have strengthened the hands of transgressors?" He replied, "You saved your life." (Talmud, *Nedarim*, 22a)

As an aside, Rabbenu Nissim mentions that Ulla told the killer to slit the throat to hasten death and alleviate agony.

Another exemption is that "One may modify a statement in the interests of peace" (*Yevamot*, 65b). According to one Talmudic view, this is not merely an option, it is mandatory.

There is also the classic instance of the bride. "How does one dance before the bride? Bet Shammai say: The bride as she is. And Bet Hillel say: Beautiful and graceful bride. (Talmud, *Ketuvot*, 16b-17a). Hillel allows even the undeserved compliment, perhaps because beauty is in the eyes of the beholder. The groom must believe that the bride is indeed beautiful, so that the statement is not untrue.

The ethical imperative to speak honestly, without deception, is a well-established norm in Judaism, in spite of all the exceptions. The extent to which integrity is lauded can be seen in Rashi's comment on the reference to Joseph's brothers as being "unable to speak peacably to him" (*Genesis*, 37:4). Rashi observes — "From their discredit we may infer something to their credit; they did not say one thing with their mouth while thinking something else in their hearts." The behaviour of Joseph's brothers was despicable. Yet, their honest refusal to speak to him deceitfully is singled out as a positive feature of an otherwise undesirable demeanor.

The Torah scholar is singled out for particular admonition. "Any Torah scholar whose inside is not like the outside is no scholar" (Talmud, *Yoma*, 72b). Another view considers such a person as abominable. The Talmud here evokes a feeling easily corroborated by daily experience. In almost every community, even one of moral or spiritual laxity, congregations will tolerate moral failings of members, but will hold no brief for any member of the clergy who indulges in questionable activities. True, they consider the clergy to be human. But they also demand some exemplary model to which they can point and whom they can respect. The possibility exists that these religious leaders serve as a form of vicarious atonement for the masses. But the fact remains that, in spite of the talk of equality and of all being human, a higher degree of integrity is expected of the leaders. Watergate points to this quite cogently. We may expect politics to have unseemly parts to it and we can live with this reality. But if the unseemliness reaches the top we do not tolerate that. However paradoxical it might be, people desire a model, an ideal, which they can emulate at the same time as they deny the desired ideal in their own lives.

The main prohibition emanating from the requirement of absolute honesty and integrity is — "It is forbidden to deceive (literally, steal the mind of) people, even gentiles" (Talmud,

Hullin, 94a). The Talmud offers some pertinent examples of deception, or mind stealing:

> A man should not urge his friend to dine with him when he knows that his friend will not do so. And he should not offer him many gifts when he knows that his friend will not accept them....And he should not invite him to anoint himself with oil if the jar is empty. (ibid.)

A THIN LINE

The line between integrity and chicanery is a thin one. The act itself is not as decisive as the intent. Regarding the prohibition against inviting one to anoint himself from an empty jar, the Talmud comments — "If, however, the purpose is to show the guest great respect, it is permitted" (ibid.). The act is the same, only the true intent separates the genuine from the false.

The Talmud also points out that there are some reasonable limits beyond which we need not concern ourselves with possible deception:

> Mar Zutra the son of Rav Nahman was once going from Sikara to Mahuza, while Raba and Rav Safra were going to Sikara, and they met on the way. Believing they had come to meet him, he said, "Why did the Rabbis take this trouble to come so far to meet me?" Rav Safra replied, "We did not know that the master was coming; had we known we would have put ourselves out more than this!" Raba said to him, "Why did you tell him this; you have now upest him?" He replied, "But we would be deceiving him otherwise!" "No. He would be deceiving himself." (ibid., 94b)

It should be noted that this is the same Rav Safra who was a model of honesty. He once had an article to sell and, while reciting the Sh'ma, a prospective buyer made an offer. Rav Safra overtly ignored him as he was in the midst of prayer. The buyer, thinking that Rav Safra had rejected the offer, upped his bid. When Rav Safra finished the Sh'ma, he gave the article for the original bid, as that was what he had intended to accept as payment for the article (Sheiltot, *Genesis*, 36).

INDIVIDUAL, FAMILY, COMMUNITY:
JUDEO-PSYCHOLOGICAL PERSPECTIVES

We must make a distinction between the intent to fool and the attitude to foolishness. The Talmud judiciously suggests that honesty is something internal, and external forces or thoughts which impute the wrong motives to innocent behaviour need not impede the spontaneous flow of normal expression. To maintain an honest posture is an ethical challenge; to ensure that everyone thinks you are honest is an experiental impossibility.

One apparent contradiction to the internality of the concept of hypocrisy is the well known adage — "Only part of a person's praise may be said in the person's presence, but all of it in the person's absence" (Talmud, *Eruvin*, 18b). Rashi's comment on this is that excessive praise appears as flattery, or dishonest acclaim. It appears so, even if the praise is honestly intended. However, it is likely that the concern with appearance has little to do with judging intent. It is assumed that the praise is sincere; the admonition to temper the acclaim is along the lines of "one who adds, subtracts" (Talmud, *Sanhedrin*, 29a). It is suggested that there is a point of diminishing returns in lauding a fellow; fulsome adjectives may, in effect, either embarrass the intended beneficiary or so discredit the effuser as to render all the pronouncements meaningless.

M'Harsha on Eruvin (18b) suggests that the reason for this might be so that one who is flattered will not become swell-headed and think of the self as great. He cites a Midrash (*Genesis Rabbah*, 32:3) where this same caution about over-effusion is mentioned regarding praise directed to God. M'Harsha rightly concludes that reasons of swell-headedness could not apply to God and thus implies that swell-headedness is not the main factor even in the human situation, as the Midrash cites the two applications in the same discussion.

It it quite obvious that Judaism places a great premium on honest, sincere expression. Even the almost pathological abhorrence of swine within Judaism can be seen as the affirmation of natural integrity and the rejection of false images. The swine is unique in that, while it is unfit to be eaten, its outward signs are the same as those of an acceptable animal. "When the swine is lying down it points out its hoofs, as if to say, `I am clean'" (*Midrash Rabbah*, Genesis 65:1). The swine thus symbolizes the projection of acceptability in spite of its falseness. In a way, then, the concept of kashrut is not so far removed from the demands of integrity.

Regarding the vacationers, eating kosher on the Shabbat flight would have been free from false projections. Like the one making the proverbial hole-in-one on Yom Kippur, whom were they going to tell? In terms of both the outward expression and the inner intent, it would not have been hypocritical at all.

The discussion until now has focused on the philosophical aspect of honesty vs. hypocrisy. At this point, it is crucial to bring the concept of mitzvah, commandment, into the picture.

INTENT AND COMMANDMENT

Travelling on Shabbat is not Shabbos-dik (consistent with the law and spirit of Shabbat); eating kosher is a bona fide fulfillment of Judaic values. Is this dualistic, spiritually schizophrenic experience an instance of immersing in a mikvah (ritual bath) with an unclean reptile in the hand, or is it a desirable avoidance of yet another transgression, a way to prevent compound error? In other words, is it a mockery to fulfill a precept at the very time of transgression?

Purity in the fulfillment of commandments is, undoubtedly, desirable. "And let all your actions be for the sake of God" (Talmud, *Avot*, 2:17). Desirability notwithstanding, it is recognized that purity may remain an abstract, distant goal not readily actualized. This is not seen as an excuse to desist from Judaic experience. Rather, "One should always occupy the self with Torah and good deeds, though it is not for their own sake, for out of doing good with an ulterior motive comes doing good for its own sake" (Talmud, *Pesahim*, 50b).

In another statement, the Talmud asserts; "If one does them for other motives, it would be better had he not been created" (*Berakhot*, 17a). *Tosafot*, in resolving this contradiction, distinguishes between the lack of purity, which is not the highest expression but is at least *on the way*, and rebellious motives, which are so despicable as to result in the Talmud's questioning the value of such existence. The concept of "on the way towards true expression" is an obvious necessity. If Judaism were to insist on absolute sincerity and true commitement from the outset, it would effectively legislate itself out of existence. If anything less than total observance were forbidden, no immersion in Jewish experience could begin. The educative process of "trying one's best" would be ruled out, and commitment would have to come almost spontaneously and completely. This is just about impossible.

The commitment made on Sinai, "We will do and we will understand," in which commitment preceded knowledge, is not a contradiction of this view. There, the overwhelmingness of the Divine presence acted as an irresistable force inducing commitment.

The problem of fulfillment which is achieved through transgression is a step beyond purity in fulfilling a commandment. Generally, one cannot fulfill a precept thorugh a trespass; for instance, a stolen lulav (palm branch) cannot be used to actualize the commandment of lulav on Sukkot (Talmud, *Sukkah*, 30a).

Granted that this is not the unanimous opinion, it nevertheless is the prevailing view.

A more pertinent situation revolves around the recitation of a brakhah, a blessing, on food which was acquired illegally.

If one stole a se'ah of wheat, kneaded it and baked it, and set aside a portion of it as hallah (priestly portion of the dough), how would he be able to pronounce the benediction? He would surely not be pronouncing a blessing but pronouncing a blasphemy. (Talmud, *Baba Kamma*, 94a)

Kesef Mishneh (Laws of Blessings, 1:19) develops this concept and how it applies to making a blessing on stolen matzah. According to *TaZ* (Orah Hayyim 196:1, note 1), *Rabad*, who argues with Maimonides and says that one can recite a blessing when eating forbidden food, applies this only to one who does so unwittingly. But one who consciously eats forbidden food cannot, even in Rabad's view, recite a blessing. TaZ consistently avers that in cases of performing a mitzvah through transgression no blessing can be made. *Orah Hayyim* (11:6, note 5) calls fringes (zizit) from stolen wool an abomination. In Orah Hayyim (25:12, note 14), TaZ holds that even after y'oosh (owners' giving up hope of

ever recovering stolen goods) and change in possession no blessing may be recited. In this he differs from Magen Avraham.

To make mention of God, or to approach God through a
blessing via pilfering makes a mockery of Judaism. Over and
above that, it implicitly establishes the commandment as the
ultimate end, the attainment of which justifies all means. Commandment and Commander are fused into one, so that, in essence,
not God is embraced; instead, the commandment is idolized.
Hence, blasphemy. The warning of the Kotzker Rebbe that a
mitzvah can become *avodah zarah*, idolatry, can be readily appreciated as no mere fiction.

TWO WRONGS

At the same time that fulfillment through sin is disavowed,
fulfillment in spite of sin is encouraged. Thus, the Talmud
elaborates:

> Why is it written, "Be not much wicked"? Must one not be
> much wicked, yet he may be a little wicked? Rather, if one
> has eaten garlic and the breath smells, shall one eat more
> garlic that the breath may smell even more? (*Shabbat*, 31b)

One transgression, or even a multitude of transgressions, is
no excuse for neglecting other fulfillments. The demands of
consistency do not apply in the realm of "wrong." The key, of
course, is causality. When the actualization of a precept is effected
through a sin, it is better to desist entirely in order to maintain the
status quo. When dealing with a commandment in isolation,
performing a mitzvah in spite of previous transgression, having
sinned is no excuse for sinning more. Why smell of garlic when
theological mouth wash is readily available?

This notion finds a most controversial expression in the
recitation of the priestly blessing, *birkhat kohanim*. Many synagogues, even Orthodox ones, have done away with the priestly
blessing as part of the liturgy on the grounds that they have no
kohen (priest) who is *shomer shabbat* (Shabbat observing). No
doubt, it is repulsive to many that they should be led in blessing by
a non-observant Jew. While it is true that in many cases it is the
kohen himself who withdraws from this priestly experience, still,

the attitude latent in the withdrawing process is, in many cases, the feeling that the congregation is uncomfortable with the unpriestly priest.

How consistent is the public attitude in this matter with the halakhic norm? Maimonides (Mishnah Torah) deals forthrightly with the situation.

> A priest who did not have any of the things that would disqualify him from *nesiat kappayim* (in effect, reciting the priestly blessing), even though he is not a sage, and is not observant, or people complain about him, or he does not handle his business righteously, he can be involved in the priestly blessing and we do not prevent him. For this is a positive commandment incumbent on every priest that is fit for the blessing, and wo do not tell a wicked person to add to his wickedness by desisting from the precepts. (*Laws of Prayer*, 15:6)

Maimonides, perhaps in anticipation of the attitude prevailing today, continues:

> And do not wonder and say, In what way can the blessing of this simpleton be useful? Because the bestowal of blessing is not   dependent on the priests but on God, as it is written, "They shall put my Name on the Children of Israel and I will bless them." The priests do as they are commanded and God in mercy blesses Israel as God sees fit. (ibid., 15:6)

The priest, in Maimonides' view, is merely a catalyst who initiates a process the end result of which, we hope, is Divine blessing. Who the priest is and how observant he may be are immaterial, for blessedness will come only by God's will. If there were a direct connection between the community representative and the chances of prayer being accepted, the standards would surely be more stringent Thus, concerning the community agent in prayer, whom we refer to today as the *hazzan*, the cantor, "We should appoint as the congregation's agent the greatest person in the congregation in wisdom and deeds" (ibid., 8:11). This attitude toward the cantor has, in all likelihood, spilled over into the priests' domain, for invalid yet understandable reasons.

The element of theological integrity, of total commitment, thus has two aspects, the personal and the public. For a representative of the community, in effect its model and focal point, sincere and consistent commitment is mandatory. In personal fulfillment, consistency and complete avowal is certianly desirable, but the neglect or negation of one precept should not be an excuse for total abdication, throwing out the baby with the mikvah water. The Jew who does not observe Shabbat can still maintain the norms of kashrut. The Jew who eats leaven on Passover can still hear the shofar (ram's horn) on Rosh Hashanah, and those who eat pork should still consider fasting on Yom Kippur (Day of Atonement).

FEELING AND ACTION

Undercutting the entire question of hypocrisy is a more complex problem — the existentialist climate prevalent today and its relation to Jewish experession.

At the same time that existentialist philosophies of Judaism abound, there are some basic issues raised in attempting to marry the two. Relevant to this discussion is the problem of the subjective state of the mitzvah-doer and the objective, even essential, commandment. Quite often one hears Jews say that they would like to embrace this or that precept, but that they are not yet "ready" for it. The vacationers were probably in the same frame of mind, the environmental conditions of their trip not being consistent with the feelings which they thought they should have when eating kosher food, or at least when specially ordering it.

The contrary view is taken in a well known 13th century work, *Sefer HaHinukh*.

Know that one is formed according to one's deeds, and one's heart and all one's thoughts follow the deeds with which one is occupied, whether good or bad. Even one completely wicked in the heart, the passion of whose inclinations is evil at all times, if the spirit be aroused and one places one's efforts and preoccupation diligently in Torah and mitzvot, even not for the sake of Heaven, still immediately one will lean toward the good and with the power of the deeds will eliminate the passion for evil, for one's heart is determined by one's deeds. And even if one be completely righteous and

72

the heart upright and sincere, desiring Torah and mitzvot, if perchance one will occupy the self constantly with shameful things, as for example if a king forced a person to work in a bad profession, in truth if one's entire preoccupation be constantly with that profession, one will eventually deviate from the righteous heart to be completely wicked, for it is known and true that one is determined according to one's deeds. (*Sefer HaHinukh*, Mitzvah 20).

The power of commandment, if not the essence of Judaism, inheres in the deed shaping the person. Sefer HaHinukh cites the following Talmudic evidence of this view: "God desired to make Israel worthy; therefore God gave to them the Torah to study and many commandments to do" (ibid.; *Makkot*, 23b)

In effect, this becomes a chicken-egg problem. Is it the person in the purity of the subjective state who should wait until ready to embrace a precept, or is it the precept and its mystical shaping power that should be embraced, precisely because one does not feel ready? The previously cited sources lean toward the latter contingency, as does the well known statement, "The precepts were given only in order that one might be refined by them" (*Midrash Rabbah*, Genesis, 44:1).

The issue raised is too vital to gloss over, but in the framework of this analysis, it is not the central issue. For our purposes, it seems that the vacationers would have been well within the mainstream of Jewish thought in ordering the kosher meals. Insofar as the question of hypocrisy is concerned, their fear that the act might seem deceitful is almost a guarantee against its really being hypocritical. It is paradoxical, yet true, that hypocrisy is usually found in those who do not seem aware of the hypocritical nature of their behaviour.

This argument must be tempered by the possibility that the hypocrite, to hide the hypocrisy, might use verbal expressions of fear that the act be interpreted as deceitful to neutralize such thoughts. A parallel situation is found in the exemption given to the groom from reciting *Sh'ma* (faith affirmation) on his wedding night (Talmud, *Berakhot*, 16a), as he is preoccupied and cannot have proper concentration for the Sh'ma. Tosafot (*Berakhot*, 17b) asserts that, in present times, since we do not concentrate properly

73

anyway, even the groom must recite the Sh'ma, for by not reading it he would be implying that normally he concentrates properly. Change in circumstances here changes a purely intended exemption into a false act.

Insofar as the purity of the commandment is concerned, the optimist would say that the kosher experience on the Shabbat flight might even initiate a "higher" state of Jewish awareness.

One motto that evolves out of this discussion is a semi-credo that speaks the language of the times for a problem of the times; "Try it; you might not like it, but it might like you."

CHAPTER 5

THE ROLE OF THE INDIVIDUAL IN JEWISH LAW

One of the unique features of classical Judaism, as it has been transmitted over the ages, is the element of *mitzvah*, commandment. Unlike other religions with which it has been indiscriminately compared, Judaism is not a faith system per se. Rather, it is a commitment to life that is rooted in and springs forward from faith. Some, such as Maimonides, even did not include faith in God as one of the 613 commandments. Faith is the base upon which Judaism is built, that which makes Judaism possible, the source which gives birth to commands, but is not a commandment.

The 613 commandments, the *mitzvot*, and their development in Talmudic literature, and subsequent condification, all of which will henceforth be referred to as the law, are the warp and woof of Judaism. No full appreciation of Judaism is possible without an understanding of the individual laws, as well as the role of law in faith.

It is possible to view law as the vehicle through which one actualizes the self, exercising responsibleness to the Creator and fulfilling one's purpose in life. Law is thus conceived as the affirmation of the individual, who becomes, by deeds and actions, the agent of personal salvation.

REUVEN P. BULKA

TENSIONS

In the course of Jewish history, there has been almost perpetual tension within the ranks regarding the law. It begins almost immediately after the Sinai experience.

In a sarcastic comment attributed to Rabbi Meir Premishlan, it is noted that, on the verse "and there Israel encamped before the mountain" (*Exodus*, 19:2), Rashi comments — "as one person and with one mind, but all their other encampments were made in a murmuring spirit and in a spirit of dissension." Rabbi Meir explains that unity prevailed before the giving of the law, but after the law was given, each individual looked upon it as their own, insisting on the validity only of their own approach. The tension continues through the forty years wandering in the desert and into the period of the Judges and Kings, with their sometimes hostile attitude to Jewish law. The Pharisees and Sadducees fan the flames in their conflicts; Karaites offer their own version of Bible interpretation; Sabbateanism negates the validity of observance amongst other things; Frankists turn moral law upside down; Reform attacks the ritual laws; even Hasidism challenges the Orthodox approach to observance.

These conflicts, bitter as they sometimes were, are almost insignificant when compared to the great cleavage in Jewish ranks following the rise of Christianity. Here the matter of law occupies center stage, as Christianity proposes vicarious atonement and salvation, with an accompanying abrogation of the law in its theology. Christianity, a seemingly less demanding religion, eventually attracts great masses, while Judaism remains a minority group expression. Judaism and Christianity clash constantly, often not on an intellectual level. Even today, all denials to the contrary, camouflaged crusades under the guise of cooperation attempt to "swing" Jews away.

This chapter will attempt to suggest a view of Jewish law which is not so much novel as it is either unknown, neglected, or obscured in the controversy over legalism.

Immanuel Kant saw Judaism as a national-political entity, which fails as a religion to inculcate the inner-appropriateness of

76

morals, but instead demands external obedience to statutes and laws. Closer to home, Martin Buber asserted:

I do not believe that *revelation* is ever a formulation of law. It is only through man in his self-contradiction that revelation becomes legislation. This is the fact of man. I cannot admit the law transformed by man into the realm of my will, if I am to hold myself ready as well for the unmediated word of God directed to a specific hour of life. (Buber, in Rosenzweig, 1955)

According to these views, the law rather than affirming the individual, represses personal development and precludes spontaneous reaction to the Divine call, reducing the individual to a halakhically programmed computer. At the risk of oversimplification, one senses in Kant and Buber a view of Jewish law as an end in itself, as the purpose and expression of life. While this is in some measure corroborated by the religious behaviour of some individuals, nevertheless it assumes a view inconsistent with the design or intent of the law.

In coming to grips with the role of the individual in Jewish law, the very all-embracingness of the law does present problems. Jewish law contains not only a full measure of *bayn adam laMakom* laws, ordinances revolving around the person and the Creator; it also projects *bayn adam la'havero* regulations, a full corpus of laws covering the legal, ethical, and moral aspects of social interaction. While such comprehensiveness is likely to evoke an expression of some chauvinistic pride, it nonetheless points to an acute problem which cannot be avoided in the present atmosphere of existentialistic pressures.

According to a leading contemporary Jewish thinker;

For Judaism sheer compliance with the Law as such was never regarded as the ultimate value, it rather represented a means to the fulfillment of the Divine Will. (Wurzburger, in Appel, 1970, p. 8)

In support of this view, one need only think of the multitude of open-ended categories in applying Jewish law. For our purposes, it will be helpful to treat separately the realms of *bayn adam*

77

laMakom, ritual law, which, for obvious reasons, I prefer to call transcending laws, and *bayn adam la'havero*, or social legislation.

WITHIN THE BOUNDARY

In the domain of social legislation, one frequently encounters the notion of *lifnim meshurat hadin* (Talmud, *Berakhot*, 7a; *Ketuvot*, 97a; *Baba Kamma*, 99b-100a; *Baba Mezia*, 24b; 30b), which is often erroneously translated as "beyond the requirements of the law." *Lifnim* actually means inside, within, suggesting a profoundly symbolic category of *within the boundary of the law*. What is proposed as social legislation in Judaism is not the *summum bonum*, the ultimate good. It is the lower, irreducible limit, the boundary line. Within the pale of the law, one oscillates between straddling the border and approaching the core, the heart and soul of the law. Straddling the border has its own dangers, including the likelihood that in straddling one may overstep, as well as the danger that the law can become a veneer, used by the individual as a camouflage for personal interests. *Lifnim* is thus recommended for legal, as well as humanistic, reasons.

The notion of *lifnim* has its counterpart in open society. There, human life, humanistic life, has self-evident boundaries beyond which resides the dimension of the animalistic. Self-evident boundaries, inhumane expressions such as theft, rape, murder, etc., are beyond the outer periphery, wherein resides something less than the human dimension. These boundaries leave wide-open areas for human expression within the perimeter. Humanness, in this settng, is not limited by boundaries, rather it is made possible by boundaries. An analogy from Viktor Frankl's concept of freedom is useful.

Certainly man is free, but he is not floating freely in airless space. He is always surrounded by a host of restrictions. These restrictions, however, are the jumping-off points for his freedom. Freedom presupposes restrictions, is contingent upon restrictions. (Frankl, 1967, p. 61)

In a parallel sense, the thrust of Judaic social legislation is towards circumscribing a frontier within which one has ample room for being oneself and expressing one's self. Thus, the

Talmud interprets the scriptural passage concerning the obligation to make known to the people the deeds *that they are to do* (*Exodus*, 18:20) as a reference to *lifnim meshurat hadin* (*Baba Kamma*, 100a), within the line of the law into the human dimension. What *they are to do*, what is an authentic expression of one's higher development, is *within* the borders of the legal framework.

Lifnim meshurat hadin is more than just a higher form of expression of Judaic law. It has already been pointed out (Belkin, 1960, pp. 190-191) that all eleven principles of virtue to which David had condensed the 613 *mitzvot* are, without exception, expressions of the notion of *lifnim meshurat hadin*.

For example, the virtue of *nor does evil to his fellow* (*Psalms*, 15:3) is interpreted beyond the passive state of not harming a neighbour. It is taken as referring to the meticulous detail one should give in order to refrain from even indirect harm. *Speaks truth in his heart* (*ibid*, 15:2) is applied to the behaviour of people like Rav Safra, who in his scrupulous adherence to the truth, refused a higher offer for an item simply because in his mind alone he had accepted the original offer. *Nor takes a bribe against the innocent* (*ibid.*, 15:5), hardly an excelling virtue, is applied to such as Rabbe Yishmael son of Rabbe Yose, who avoided even the slightest possibility of conflict of interest in deference to the purity of judicial inquiry (Talmud, *Makkot*, 24a).

At least in the realm of social legislation, where the concept of *lifnim meshurat hadin* is applicable, Judaism seems to posit a strong dose of human contribution.

Lifnim meshurat hadin is applied mainly in social situations, such as property rules, when one should return property even though not required by law. An exception is that of *Berakhot* 45b, where it is stated — "If three persons have been eating together, one breaks off (eating) to oblige two, but two do not break off to oblige one. But do they not? Did not Rav Papa break off for Abba Mar his son, he and another with him? Rav Papa was different because he went *lifnim meshurat hadin*." Whilst this deals with the question of *zimun* (reciting grace together), which is not in the category of social law, nevertheless, the matter of two waiting for one, or breaking off for one is really a question of social ethics; even here *lifnim meshurat hadin* is a social expression.

REUVEN P. BULKA

The ultimate importance attached to this concept is seen in the Talmudic assertion that one of the reasons why Jerusalem had to be destroyed is "because they based their judgements (strictly) upon Biblical law, and did not go *lifnim meshurat hadin (Baba Mezia,* 30b). *Tosafot* (ad. loc.) questions this from another Talmudic statement attributing the destruction to wanton hate. He answers that both were causes. One could also suggest that wanton hate and strict application of the law are related and interwoven with each other. The lack of feeling for another is often masked in mercilessly applying strict law, with no demonstration of kindness. The law perfunctorily observed, albeit even scrupulously, is not authentic Judaism. Judaism demands the individual.

Lifnim meshurat hadin does not exhaust the categories in social legislation where virtue depends on the individual. There are such other notions as *midot hasidut* (Talmud, *Shabbat,* 120a; *Baba Mezia,* 52b; *Hullin,* 130b), the way of the pious; *lazet yeday Shamayim* (Talmud, *Shabbat,* 120a; *Gittin,* 53a; *Baba Kamma,* 56a; 98a; *Baba Mezia,* 37a), fulfilling the dictates of Heaven; *v'aseeta hayashar v'hatov* (*Deuteronomy,* 6:18; *Baba Mezia,* 16b; 108a; *Avodah Zarah,* 25a), doing that which is right and good; and *l'maan telekh b'derekh tovim* (*Proverbs,* 2:20; Talmud, *Baba Mezia,* 83a), to walk in the way of good people. These categories do not lend themselves to a legal framework. Instead they function *within* the legal framework in accordance with the ethical growth of the individual. For the Jew, sensitivity and conscience development, tightly bounded by the full gamut of social legislation, is given more than ample room to mature. God's word can go only so far. After that it is up to the individual to take up the baton, to give meaning and life to the body of laws with one's heart and soul. Here enforceable Judaism ends and the responsive human enters.

TRANSCENDING LAW

Beyond social legislation, the next step is to comprehend the thrust of transcending legislation, the *bayn adam laMakom* (between the individual and God) laws. Whereas in the social realm the construct is, to a large extent, one-dimensional, in that the law serves to thrust the individual into the core, away from the outer border; in the transcending ordinances, the *mitzvot* function in terms of one's dialogue with God, propelling the individual into the dimension of transcendence. As a note of caution, though this dimensional picture is true to some extent, it should be borne in mind that every *bayn adam la'havero* (between the individual and one's fellow) law has an element of *bayn adam laMakom* in it, and every *bayn adam laMakom* command has potential feedback into the social situation.

Again, reference to a Franklian analogy is useful.

The ground upon which man walks is always being transcended in the process of walking, and serves as ground only to the extent that it is transcended, that it provides a springboard. (Frankl, 1967, p. 61)

In the domain of transcending legislation, attention will be focused on how the law serves as a springboard to literally propel the individual into a transcending dimension.

An illustration is helpful. The commandments regarding the Shabbat are perhaps the most minute and exacting in the vast expanse of Jewish law. Yet the great preponderance of laws are geared mainly toward interpreting the prohibitive aspect of Shabbat, the *shamor (Deuteronomy,* 5:12) component. As for the *zakhor (Exodus,* 20:8) component, the positive human contribution to the day, each individual, in his or her unique situation, decides how to best parlay Shabbat into a meaningful experience. The law is here extremely restrictive. It divorces the individual almost totally from materially creative concerns (Fromm, 1957, pp. 242-249). But in cutting off all these options, the law forces the individual into a higher dimension, where one's concerns are purely intellectual and spiritual. Shabbat still remains, paradoxically, the subject of more laws than most other precepts, and, at the same time, a symbol of *human* freedom.

This may be the message in the famous Rabbinic statement, "'Remember' and 'keep' (*zakhor* and *shamor*) were spoken in a single utterance'" (*Rosh Hashanah,* 27a). There would be no purpose to the restrictedness of *shamor* without the fulfillment in freedom of *zakhor;* hence *shamor* could not have existed, philosophically, even one second without *zakhor.* And, the fulfillment of *zakhor* would have been impossible without the bounded guidelines established by *shamor.* Hence, *zakhor* could not have existed, philosophically, even one second without *shamor*. Thus, one utterance, or mutual dependency.

As an aside, one senses in the constant challenging questions hurled at Rabbis - Why can't I drive?, Why can't I switch on a light?, Why can't I watch television?, an attitude which obviously negates the primary thrust of Shabbat law. If Shabbat laws are spring-boards, these questions testify that many people are still grounded. There is a significant gap between the person who experiences true Shabbat and the one who questions Shabbat. This difference is rarely overcome in an intellectual manner, and is best countered with the suggestion — 'try it.'

Even more radical than Shabbat in its restrictiveness is *Yom Kippur*, the Day of Atonement. Superimposed upon all those restrictions which pertain to a regular Shabbat are new ordinances dictating abstinence from eating, drinking, washing, etc. But these regulations are not intended as merely an exercise in abstinence, as is evident from the procedure followed in public fasting. The elder would address the fasting community in the following manner:

> Our brethren, neither sackcloth nor fastings are effective but only penitence and good deeds, for we find that of the men of Nineveh Scripture does not say, And God saw their sackcloth and fasting, but, "God saw their works that they turned from their evil way." (Talmud, *Ta'anit*, 16a)

This, of course, echoes the message of the prophet which is read as the Haftorah (Prophetic reading) on Yom Kippur morning.

> Is such the fast that I have chosen? The day for a man to afflict his soul? Is it to bow down his head as a bullrush, and to spread sackcloth and ashes under him? Will you call this a fast, and an acceptable day to the Lord? Is not this the fast that I have chosen? To loose the fetters of wickedness, to undo the bands of the yoke....Is it not to deal your bread to the hungry and that you bring the poor that are cast out to your house..." (*Isaiah*, 58:5-71)

Fasting is not the ultimate value on Yom Kippur. R. Elimel-ekh of Lizhensk, when asked to explain why the Baal Shem Tov fasted, replied that when the Baal Shem was young he would go into seclusion for an entire week with six loaves of bread and water. Upon interrupting his meditation on Friday to return home, he would lift up his sack, and, not understanding why it was so heavy, would be surprised to find his loaves still there. Such fasting, said R. Elimelekh, is allowed (Buber, 1958, p. 45).

Through fasting, however, one is divorced not only from material creativity, but also from any immediate material concerns. One is then forced into a purely spiritual dimension, where the concerns are self-investigation, confrontation with responsibility, acknowledgement of previous failings, and, in the spirit of *teshuvah* - repentance, resolution for the future. To be sprung into the spiritual realm, the law, in its exacting stringency, ordains a negation of the material. One's response to this situation, as in the case of Shabbat, is facilitated by law, but not programmed by law. Each individual's *teshuvah* is a reflection of the peculiar position and nature of the *baal teshuvah* (penitent).

It is possible to view the setting of Passover, with its accent on reliving the Exodus experience at the onset of Jewish history, as a call to appreciate the implications of the event for the present moment, or to investigate the freedom of one's immediate situation. The absence of any particular transcending observance on *Shavuot* over and above the normal *Yom Tov* regulations serves to set the day aside to relive the Sinai experience. It signifies the mystical and intellectual emotion of being addressed by a revelation, at the present moment. This might seem homiletical, but in attempting to project the role of the individual in transcending law, the dividing line between philosophy and homiletics is blurred, if not obscured.

In the realm of experience, Jewish law manifests its concern not only in advocating the experience; it also creates, through the mechanism of prohibitive commandments, the setting in which such experience is not only possible, but also evoked.

THE HUMAN INGREDIENT

The role of the individual does not end here. In the exercise of prayer, where the matter of prescribed textual entreaties is a controversial topic, the Talmud asserts; "If one makes prayer a fixed task, it is not a (genuine) supplication" (*Berakhot*, 28b). By fixed task the Talmud means, according to one view, the prayer which is looked upon as a burden (*ibid.*, 29b). The attitude one has in approaching a commandment is of singular importance. Prayer pronounced as a task, a burden, is not the desired expression. Lacking the proper motivation, it becomes a rote exercise, something less than sincere prayer.

Attitude plays a major role in other situations. Regarding the honour due to parents, the Talmud says the following:

> One may give his father pheasants as food, yet (this) drives him from the world; whereas another may make him grind in a mill and (this) brings him to the world to come. (*Kiddushin*, 31a-b)

The difference here is between one who performs a duty, but grudgingly, and another, who cannot do what is really desired, but does whatever possible with love. In the Talmudic view, "Charity is rewarded only according to the kindness accompanying it" (*Sukkah*, 49b). The Talmud recognized that while machines can coin money, only humans can transmit concern. Within the legal framework, concern cannot be quantified and is not an enforceable category, but the ultimate value of the deed is again dependent on the individual human contribution. The deed is the structure which effects human response. In fact, as much as in deed, structure is considered necessary. Yet there is recognition that where the value of the deed has been elicited without actualization of the deed, the purpose has been realized. Thus,

> Even if one (merely) thinks of performing a precept but is forcibly prevented, the Writ ascribes it to him as though he has performed it. (Talmud, *Kiddushin*, 40a)

In the view of transcending law as springboard, even the sincere desire to fulfill a *mitzvah* propels the individual into the transcending dimension.

In the area of attitudes, there is an almost inexhaustible number of categories which are distinctly human contributions. As examples, the following may be cited: *v'anvayhu* (Talmud, *Shabbat*, 133b; *Sukkah*, 11b; *Nazir* 2b), adorning the precepts; *hidur mitzvah* (Talmud, *Baba Kamma*, 9b), beautifying the commandment; *hivuv mitzvah* (Talmud, *Pesahim*, 68b; *Sukkah*, 41b; *Sotah*, 13a; *Kiddushin*, 33a), love of the commandment; *lishmah* (Talmud, *Pesahim*, 38b; 50b; *Sukkah*, 9a; *Gittin*, 20a; *Avodah Zarah*, 27a), the intent for fulfilling the precept; *kavanah* (Talmud, *Berakhot*, 5b; 13a; 31a; *Eruvin*, 95b; *Pesahim*, 114b; *Megillah*, 20a), single-mindedness in fulfilling the command; *zerizut* (Talmud, *Pesahim*, 89b; *Yoma*, 84b; *Menahot*, 43b), eagerness to fulfill the ordinance. Some combination of various of these categories is imperative to make *mitzvah* a meaningful endeavour. The proper attitude in fulfilling law is expressed with these means of approach, which are normally linked to the transcending laws, though many can be equally applied to social laws.

As a further indication that transcending laws are deficient, that they miss the point when performed mechanistically, Isaiah castigates the people because their fear of God "is a commandment of men learned by rote" (29:13). The commentary of RaDaK is instructive. He explains; "*learned by rote*, because one who does only what is commanded and does not add of his own, does not do because he really wants or wills to." In simple terms, the law is the jumping-off point, and the real spirit of the law is captured by adding human ingredients to it. The prophet condemns the programmed Jew, who may be perfunctorily exact but who has thus reduced the self to a lifeless person, not responding to situations in the freedom and spontaneity of human conscience within the guidelines of Judaism.

The classic Talmudic definition of a *hasid shoteh*, foolish pietist, who is considered a destructive force, is one who sees a woman drowning in the river and yet proclaims, "It is improper for me to look upon her and rescue her" (*Sotah*, 21b). This reveals an awareness of the distortions that arise from one's interpreting law as the ultimate reality, in the process projecting stringency upon stringency to the point of denying life. Perhaps this is what the Hasidic sage had in mind when he cautioned his followers that one man can make idolatry even out of commandment.

Finally, it would be appropriate to introduce the concept of *averah lishmah* (Talmud, *Nazir*, 23b), a transgression performed with good intention. As the law is generally directed towards an affirmation of life, it is recognized that at times one might transgress for a greater value. To be sure, *carte blanche* in this circumstance is not forthcoming, but the mere existence of the notion is itself meaningful. Also, it is paralleled by the famous charge, "live thereby" (*Leviticus*, 18:5), on which is based the right of the individual to transgress in order to preserve life. If the law, properly understood, is for the individual and for life, a clash with life militates strongly in favour of disregarding a precept in order to preserve life. The law is but a means. If it is made an end, or if one would face one's end because of it, the law, with few exceptions (Talmud, *Sanhedrin*, 74a), humbly withdraws itself temporarily.

THE MEANS

It would seem ridiculous to even suggest that Judaism is legalistic. In allowing the Torah and Talmud to speak for themselves, it appears perfectly obvious that it is not in the law, but rather (in social legislation) *within* and (in transcending legislation) *through* the law that authentic Judaism is expressed. The law is the carefully constructed framework to elicit the highest level of one's social and spiritual essence.

Given the role of the law as means, nevertheless it remains historically correct that, every so often, Jews fall into a rut wherein the law becomes the end itself. In the 18th century the Hasidim said of their opponents, the Mitnagdim, that they were afraid of transgressing against the Code of Law, while they, the Hasidim, were in fear of transgressing against God. In reaction to this, the Hasidim continue to emphasize, and sometimes even overemphasize, not the command per se, but how it is observed. It is healthy to be reminded every so often of the true nature of Jewish law. In the words of Rav, "The precepts were given only in order that people might be refined by them. For what does the Holy One, blessed be God, care whether one kills an animal by the throat or by the nape of its neck?" (*Midrash Rabbah*, Genesis, 44:1)

Today the tables are turned somewhat. Quite possibly, in their zealousness, the spiritual heirs of the Hasidic movement have lost sight of their own message — that the law is a means, not an end. Granted this oversimplifies matters, but it is hard to suppress the feeling that were these people, indeed everyone, to re-acknowledge that the Jew does not exist for the sake of

Halakhah, rather Halakhah exists for the sake of the Jew, the spiritual condition of Israel would be much more harmonious.

SECTION TWO

THE FAMILY

CHAPTER 6

THE FAMILY: A JEWISH TROUBLE SPOT

The ongoing concern within the Jewish community for the fate of the family is an expression both of concern for the Jewish community and for the future of Judaism. Historically, the genesis of Judaism is in the family. The humble beginnings of Judaism were with a father and his four wives, their twelve children, and the ensuing extended family, which moved as a group to a new location, expanded, proliferated, was redeemed, and then, as a collective family, accepted its responsibilities.

Other religions worked in the reverse. A prophet or a redeemer, claiming to have received a directive from God, shared this message with disciples who would gather up more followers either voluntarily or by force. The revelation came first and the family of followers, second. In Judaism the family came first; the revelation was directed to an existent family.

This societal-theological evolution of Judaism is linked to the conception of Judaism as a *way of life* emanating from monotheistic faith, rather than being the mere affirmation of faith. As a way of life, it flourishes when lived out in an harmonious environment. For a long time the extended family, extending into a community, or shtetl, was most conducive to and appropriate for actualizing one's Jewishness.

Although there are a number of shtetl-like Jewish communities in North America, shtetl life today is more a fact of history than a sociological prospect. The realities of the North American lifestyle are with us. Solutions to whatever problems may be confronting the Jewish family must be found within the context of the existing structure.

This presentation will depict the philosophies and sociological patterns unfolding in the North American community in general and their affect on the Jewish Community. Five distinct areas which affect Jewish family life will be examined: (1) lifestyle, (2) divorce and single parenthood, (3) fertility, (4) intermarriage and (5) women's role.

LIFESTYLE

The many problems that face the family today can be attributed, in large measure, to a new ethic which has pervaded America, the ethic of self-realization. This ethic emphasizes the individual's search for the self above all other considerations. The glorification of the self has brought with it a capacity to rationalize personal decisions which may either prevent the creation of, or undo existing families. This narcissism or self-realization ethic — the me generation — may be seen as the natural extension of a philosophical world view which posits the human *right* "to life, liberty and the pursuit of happiness."

Life is defined in terms of individual needs and how they may be fulfilled. One marries an individual who fills personal needs, has children in order to fulfill the procreative urge, joins the work force to find oneself. This almost one-sided search for the self often neglects the needs of others and creates insular lifestyles accentuating privacy; space and time for oneself.

People value privacy as if it were their most prized possession. Our family structures betray the primacy of privacy. We live in private homes or semi-private homes, hospitals have private rooms or semi-private rooms, as if the element of privacy with whatever adjective preceding it is a guage of what is good. But privacy comes at a very painful price, the price of not having others when the need for companions is keenly felt. Hence the proliferation of a unique twentieth century epidemic, the ubiquitous manifestation of loneliness (see chapter 3).

The home structure which has evolved in North America has resulted in a new phenomenon. Holt points out that this is certainly not the first generation in which children must have a working relationship with their parents, but it is the first generation in which children must have a working relationship *only* with their parents. The penchant for privacy has just about locked everyone else out from being a significant life-force in the child's development. Phillippe Aries aptly describes the modern family as a "prison of love," where the child *has* to get along with the parent, or else. It is not surprising that in such a pressure cooker, feelings of guilt should arise and feelings of hostility, if repressed in the home, are vented in other environments, most notably the schools. What are developing are not so much nuclear families as potential nuclear explosions.

No one seems to have enough of that most precious commodity — time. Parents do not have enough time to teach their children, to enjoy with their children. What previously were home responsibilities are now parcelled out. Whereas in previous times Jewish education was transmitted through living example and through joyful parent-child experiences, this aspect of the child's development is often relegated to specialists in the field, teachers. Even the initial years of a child's development are increasingly becoming the responsibility of daycare centers (Bronfenbrenner, 1977). Fathers and mothers are generally spending less and less time with their children. Uri Bronfenbrenner calculated a little while ago that the average father spends about twenty minutes per day with his child, of which only 38 seconds is true intimate contact. This is certainly not enough to induce a child to feel a sense of rootedness in the world and warmth in the home environment.

With all the talk of the single parent family, it should be observed that there are many families made up of a husband, wife and children, which are, effectively, either single parent or even parentless. The finding of Bronfenbrenner that one third of all mothers with children under three are working and that an increasing number of children are coming home to empty houses indicates that the symptoms of single parent families may prevail in many more households than statistics indicate. In terms of the potential dangers this portends, Bronfenbrenner indicates that children coming home to empty houses is as reliable a predicter as any for such future troubles as dropping out, depression and addiction.

DIVORCE AND SINGLE PARENTHOOD

The ethic of self-realization has been implicated by a leading sociologist, Robert Weiss (1975), as a prime factor in the increasing divorce rate, which hovers between 30% and 40% and, if trends continue, may rise to somewhere close to 50%. Weiss contends that in all the divorces with which he has been involved, the ethic of self-realization has been an important factor in the split, if not the primary factor.

Divorce or separation is not the only cause of single parenthood. Approximately 54% of single parenthood is related to divorce or separation, but 40% of single parenthood is related to the death of the spouse. Single parenthood has become an accepted fact of life in America, so much so that in a recent survey, 74% of Americans said it is morally acceptable to be single and to have children.

Of course, single parenthood which results from the death of a spouse cannot be avoided by any social strategies, but divorce is a different issue. Using data from the National Opinion Research Center study of 1973 to 1975, Glenn and Weaver point out that 71% of men who have never divorced say they are happy in their marriages and 68% of remarried men describe themselves as very happy in their marriages. For women there is a slightly greater gap, in that 70% of never divorced women say they are happily married, and only 61% of formerly divorced women say they are happily married (1978). The reasons for this difference are open to conjecture, but it is clear that there is nothing permanently problematic in individuals who divorce. They show a resilience, an ability to bounce back. Indeed, almost 80% of those who divorce do remarry, and the fact that it works the second time around leads one to question whether the first divorce was really necessary.

A study of divorce (*Berry*, 1978) in Wisconsin showed that approximately one out of every ten divorces should never have taken place, based on the feelings of the former spouses months after the finalization of the divorce. Have we been too liberal in accepting divorce as *the* escape hatch for a marriage which does not work? The more people divorce, the more it becomes accepted, and the less likely a couple will be to work their problems out when confronted with a crisis.

A study by Leo Davids (1982) estimated that in 1977 there were 1,000 divorces amongst Jewish families in Canada, with the likelihood that the years following 1977 were no better, and probably worse. According to Ben Schlesinger, there are approximately 9,000-10,000 single parent Jewish families in Canada and between 13,500-15,000 children who are being either mothered or fathered by a single parent (1983). Considering that the U.S. Jewish population is about ten times that of Canada, one can project, in rough approximation, the number of single parent Jewish families in the U.S.

The proliferation of single parent families will continue to test the resources of the Jewish community. Especially when the split emanates from divorce, the fallout has repercussions which go beyond the immediate family. The increasing rate of divorce has the effect of rupturing family ties and forces the families of the divorcing couple into a "them versus us" confrontation. In the long run this can have a devastating affect on the cohesiveness of the Jewish community. It is, therefore, imperative for the community to learn how to live with divorce peacefully, rather than to let it escalate into mini-wars pitting family factions against each other.

The situation of single parenthood often detaches the parent and children from any meaningful contact with the community, so that the experience of Jewishness often diminishes in many of these families. On the other hand, many single parents send their children to day school while they work, since the day school starts earlier, ends later, and therefore offers more convenient child care. Additionally, many single parents, because of the economic burdens thrust upon them, go back home to their own parents. Parents are often a source of partisan support during the marital crisis and it is not unlikely that in the economic pinch which follows, the older generation family is leaned on again. This has its obvious disadvantages for those who crave privacy, but in an ironic way it brings families back together in an extended set-up.

95

This is happening across North America for economic reasons, not only in single parent families, but even amongst marrieds.

It is important for the community to create imaginative Jewish living programs which integrate the single parent family into a communal structure which, up until how, has been almost exclusively oriented towards the two parent family. Day care centers for children of single parents, as for children of two parent families, are an important area where Jewish values may be shared in a happy environment. Single parenthood can be a stimulus to greater Jewish involvement rather than a harbinger of spiritual attrition. Some even recommend that children of single parents be allowed to attend day schools free of tuition. Such a move, noble as it sounds, may be counter-productive, as it may encourage "mock separations."

FERTILITY

Any discussion of the Jewish family must involve a discussion of reproduction. Fertility trends, too, have fallen prey to the "ethic of self-realization" syndrome. In general, Americans have veered away from an emphasis on family life. More people are either remaining single or living together. A relatively recent survey showed that more than 50% of Americans feel there is nothing morally wrong with living together when not married. This, I guess, is not the common idea of a moral majority. Only 37% condemn pre-marital sex as morally wrong (Yankelovich, 1981, pp. 94; 92).

In 1957, 80% of those surveyed felt that women who remain unmarried must be either sick, neurotic, or immoral. By 1978 only 25% felt that way. This may be due to a more precise appreciation of what it means to be neurotic or sick, but in line with other findings, it also indicates a more liberal view towards the need to be married and to procreate. Fewer and fewer people, only 16% of the population, feel that four or more children is the ideal family size; 51% feel that two children is the ideal (Yankelovich, 1981, p. 91).

This liberal attitude has spilled over into the Jewish community, in extremis. The estimated fertility rate amongst Jews is 1.7

per family, meaning that we are wrestling not with zero population growth, but negative population growth. More Jews opt for never marrying, perhaps scared off by the rising rate of divorce and the tales of woe shared by victims of divorce.

In Boston, for example, only 27% of the adult population was not married in 1965, but by 1975 fully 44% of the adult Jewish population was not married. In the 21-29 age grouping, the percentage of those married tailed off from 58% in 1965 to 42% in 1975 (Waxman, 1982). Additionally, aside from the living together syndrome, some are either marrying late or marrying early and holding off from having children, either to pursue a career or for fear the marriage may not work out and they would rather not be stuck with children. The lateness of the childbearing age often precludes having more than one or two children. Besides this, many couples would not have wanted more than one or two in any event.

It is questionable whether the quality of family life is affected by its size. Some people feel that a larger family has more interaction and sharing of roles and therefore is a more viable entity. Others maintain that a single child may have the advantage of individual attention and develop into a better rounded personality. The fact remains that low fertility rates do not bode well for the future of the Jewish community. With the already alarming attrition caused by intermarriage, compounded by a negative population growth, the size of the Jewish community of the future will be diminished. This will compromise the strength of a community which gleans much from numerical strength and closeness.

INTERMARRIAGE

The me generation is no doubt involved in the intermarriage dilemma facing the North American Jewish community. Elazar's (1976) survey of the American Jewish community found 25% to 30% of the population totally uninvolved in Jewish life. Elazar called these people "peripherals." Then there are the "contributors and consumers," who identify with the community but are only minimally associated, again numbering between 25% and 30%. At the very least, then, at least half the American Jewish population is tenuously bound up with Jewish destiny. The rate of intermarriage, when viewed in the background of Elazar's findings, should hardly be surprising. It is generally believed that in the United States the intermarriage rate hovers around 35% to 40% (Massarik, n.d.). More alarming is the finding in the National Jewish Population study of 1971 that fully 43% of all American Jews feel there is nothing wrong with intermarriage, and amongst the then 20 to 29 year-olds, 69% felt it is okay for a Jew to marry a non-Jew (ibid.). In Canada, based on the Statistics Canada release of 1978, the intermarriage rate is just short of 40%. This is pure intermarriage with no conversion. If one included marriages following conversion, the rate would probably be closer to 45% or 50% (Bulka, 1981).

Intermarriage is merely a symptom, a manifestation of a sense of detachment from the Jewish community. In some cases, the prevailing attitude is that present satisfaction, that omnipresent ethic of self-realization, takes precedence over any long range commitment to Judaism or the Jewish people. The pleasures of the moment are much more important than matters of ultimate concern.

The implications of a growing intermarriage rate for family life are obvious. It has been found that the intermarrieds have weak family ties, but it is unclear whether the weak family ties lead to the intermarriage or the intermarriage creates weak family ties. Probably both are true. In my own experience, intermarriage, when it involves conversion, may bring the husband and wife together, but the parents of the married couple remain far apart. The Judaic support base of a grandparent generation for the children is compromised, if not totally destroyed, by the intermarriage. The qualitative effects of this on the next generation of Jews in North America will probably not be clear for some time. But the prognosis is not encouraging.

WOMEN'S ROLE

There has been much debate about the affect of women's liberation on the family. Changes in women's position within the family are well known. For example, whereas in 1938 75% of the American population disapproved of women earning money if the husband was capable of supporting her, in 1978 only 26% felt this way. Whereas in 1970 only 33% believed that both sexes have the responsibility for caring for their small children, in 1980 55% believed it (Yankelovich, 1981). This second finding is most encouraging. Women joining the work force has created the need for balanced parental responsibility and has pushed the husband into a more significant parenting role, at least theoretically.

A study by Bahr and Day (1978) implies that it is not working women which affects the family as much as the attitude of the women who work. If work for women is an escape from the family it can be harmful, but if it is an expression of responsibility for the family, then it need not be an impediment to the family's flourishing.

There are many interesting developments in attitudes about work itself. From 1947 to 1977 the number of men in their prime working years who dropped out of the work force doubled. Attitudes are changing. In 1969, 58% felt that hard work always pays off. By 1976, only 43% were so inclined. In 1970, one-third of the population felt that work is the center of their life. By 1978 only 14% felt this way (Yankelovich, 1981, p. 92). Women who embark on careers out of necessity may eventually find work to be the drain and bore men have already found it to be. They may reduce their emphasis on work, and reaffirm family values. Thus, what seems a threat to the family is not necessarily so.

Within the Jewish community the higher rate of unmarrieds and lower fertility rate are probably somewhat related to the new role of women, but the developing attitudes to work may neutralize this effect. For the present, however, the feeling persists that the new role assumed by women has not enhanced Jewish family life.

ASSESSMENT

On balance, some of the trends within North American society do not auger well for the future of the family. Simultaneously, what is true of North America in general usually impinges, sometimes with even greater impact, on the Jewish community. Nevertheless, certain factors need be taken into account when assessing the present and future of the Jewish family and Jewish community. The family still remains a potent social institution in North America. It is, in the words of Mary Jo Bane, "here to stay."

Additionally, the swing to the right in North America has brought with it the espousal of a return to oldtime values, one of which is a strong family.

With all the threats to the Jewish family, the resilience of the family is also in evidence. Even extended family structures in the form of havurot are sprouting in many major North American cities. The very concern for the family all across North America is also a good omen. The creation of a crisis atmosphere, even if it may be partially manufactured, can only help to sharpen the focus and strengthen the resolve to solidify the family as *the* basic component of the Jewish community.

In a number of areas, a collective effort by those in positions of influence within the Jewish community can enhance the future of the family and thus ensure Jewish continuity. A balanced combination of philosophy and policy is essential in this regard. Those who shape Jewish minds should not shrink from sharply attacking, both from the philosophical and practical viewpoint, the ethic of self-realization. There is enough evidence to show that this ethic does not even serve the interests of the self-realizers.

The ethic of self-transcendence, the notion of sharing and outer-directed concern, should be encouraged as the essential dynamic in human relations, especially husband-wife and parent-child relations. One gives up a little bit of the self in order to better the lot of others, but in that process an entire environment is enhanced, and often to the benefit of the self-transcenders.

The notion of outer-directed concern can be enlarged to incorporate the notion of marriage as expressing a shared destiny with one's partner-in-life. This is best developed in a coherent Jewish lifestyle which has a futuristic focus and in which marriage is oriented towards the ultimate destiny of the Jewish people. Shared destiny as a reason for sharing a life together is a frequently missing ingredient in Jewish marriage. Reintroducing this ingredient into Jewish marriage is obviously dependent upon reintroducing the notion of Jewish destiny as a principle of communal life, in general. Israel's precarious position, the spread of anti-semitism, the showing of "Holocaust" and "Masada," etc., have made the issue of "Jewish Destiny" much more relevant and crucial. If this is firmly established as a principle, the family will become more entrenched as the prime focus of Jewish destiny, with siginficant impact upon fertility and intermarriage, two crucial factors in the Jewish community's future.

Secondly, as people become increasingly skeptical about the fulfillment from one's work, it is vital to stress the fulfillment which accrues from devoting oneself to inner space, the home environment. The fulfillment gained from a family flourishing in a happy environment is at least as rewarding and vital as getting a raise or a promotion.

POLICY

In terms of policy, the emphasis on inner space need not be restricted to the home. Inner space can include the various places of communal gathering which are homey in spite of their size, and are oriented around an extended family. The synagogue and community center can serve as agents for bringing diverse components of the Jewish community back within the communal matrix. The extended families can also help make single parent families feel more at ease and at home within the community. And, if proper attention is given to the 50% who are only peripherally involved, they too can be part of a "broadening of the base" for the Jewish community of tomorrow.

Although the practice of helping others is usually expressed on an individual basis, the policy-making of the community should be geared towards the collective whole. Nowhere is this as important as in the community's concern for the elderly, who, because of various trends, are becoming a larger segment of the general population. It is in the community's long range interest not to see the elderly as an isolated group which needs to be cared for separately, but rather as a vital component to be integrated into the community. The entire community can benefit from the sagacity and experience of the elderly, even as they are slowed down by the more relaxed pace of the older generation. Integrating the ages into the community is so important for a younger generation which, in Bronfenbrenner's words, often does not see an older person until the late teens.

It should be realized that through intergenerational interaction both the young and the elderly become enriched. The elderly benefit from the attention given to them by the young, and the young get a definite sense of involvement and self-worth through the smiles and radiance they bring to the faces of the elderly, not to mention the wisdom they acquire.

I recently visited the University of Hartford. The university purchased a senior citizens residence with the thought of transforming it into a dormitory facility for its students. However, the senior citizens loudly protested this certain eviction. The university was forced to backtrack and allow those senior citizens who occupied apartments to remain, while the other rooms were filled with university students. Amazingly, this integration has done wonders both for the students and for the elderly in that home. The students relate very well to the elderly, care for them, and are invited to their homes for meals. The elderly, being on campus, often attend courses as part of the university's attempt to bring them into the university setting. What happened at the University of Hartford, with proper policies and direction, can happen in any North American community, and certainly in any Jewish community. Margaret Mead's recommendation of three generational communities housed together is one possibility, but variations abound.

In the end, we are to a certain extent accidents of societal trends over which we have no control. But at the same time we do have some say in the direction of our lives. We can protest philosophies, and working within the inescapable constraints thrust upon us, we can make the best of situations and often transmute them to our advantage. Jewish history is a history of reaching the seemingly unreachable and attaining the seemingly unattainable. With collective resolve as its primary resource, this generation can write a significant chapter in this glorious history. We can achieve much, even in the face of adversity, so that the family, and ultimately the community, will be strengthened and perpetuated.

CHAPTER 7

WOMEN'S ROLE: SOME ULTIMATE CONCERNS

Women's Liberation is generally acknowledged to be the leading social movement of our day. Like any movement, it has a moderate wing, a more militant wing, and a radical wing. While it would seem that the desires of the feminists are very clear, some argue that "The liberationists have no idea where their program would take us" (Gilder, 1975, p. 7).

MARRIAGE UNDER ATTACK

The Women's Liberation Movement is questioning the institutions upon which society is based. Marriage is attacked as being detrimental to women. According to Jessie Bernard,

> Because women have to put so many more eggs in the one basket of marriage, they have more of a stake in its stability. Because their happiness is more dependent on marriage than men's, they have to pay more for it. All the studies show that women make more concessions. (Gornick and Moran, 1972, p. 149)

Bernard reports that more married than single women were bothered by feelings of depression, did not feel happy most of the time, disliked their present jobs, sometimes felt they were about to go to pieces, were more afraid of death and more bothered by pains and ailments, and were more likely to be terrified by windstorms (Bernard, *ibid*, pp. 150-151). Condemning marriage for those reasons is as logical as condemning the soap industry because you see a child playing in the mud. It is based on the "sick model" rather than on the "healthy model."

Studies by Pauline Bart show that middle-aged Jewish women are twice as likely to suffer from depression when their children leave home as non-Jewish mothers (Bart, in Gornick and Moran, 1972, p. 178). Ostensibly this is an extension of the "so many more eggs in the one basket of marriage" syndrome. Bart also found that women who assume the traditional family role as housewives are not overly aggressive, and those who accept the traditional norms are more likely to respond with depression when their children leave (Bart, *ibid.*, p. 184). But these women are also found to be overprotective with their children! (Bart, *ibid.* p. 178).

In effect, Bart uses the "sick model" as a measuring rod, somewhat like Barnard. Indeed, the observations of Bernard and Bart point out the general failure of psychology in this and other areas. "Psychology has nothing to say about what women are really like, what they need, and what they want, essentially because psychology does not know" (Weisstein, in Gornick and Moran, 1972, p. 209).

This failure of psychology is admittedly not restricted to women, as Weisstein readily admits. Complicating matters is the view of Weisstein, which is shared by others, that a person's self-image is a function of what other people expect it to be (Weisstein, *ibid*, p. 210).

The failings of psychology in knowing what people are really like, or perhaps the way they should be, is illustrated in the famous study of H.J. Eysenck, who found that as far as neurotics are concerned, psychoanalysis effected an improvement rate of 44%, psychotherapy effected an improvement rate of 64%, and "no treatment at all" effected an improvement rate of 72% (Eysenck,

1952, pp. 319-324). Psychology thrives, but obviously the people they are attempting to get back on even keel do not!

All this might be easily attributed to the fact that the world of the clinic is not a healthy world, so that any philosophy which emanates from it must be slightly jaundiced. Erikson claimed that the psychoanalytic view of women is largely reconstructed from women patients who are necessarily at odds with their womanhood and the predicament to which this seemed to doom them (Erikson, 1964).

Erikson's observation is quite pertinent in realistically weighing the evidence that is usually projected by the feminists to justify their cause.

Bernard, in her studies, found that differences between married and unmarried women concerning their depression, dislike, and unhappiness, increased with age, suggesting that marriage has a traumatic effect on personality (Bernard, *op. cit.*, p. 153). Bernard theorizes that the disappointment may be explained by the fact that these women thought they were the major part of their husbands' lives when they got married. Soon they began to find out that their husbands' work comes first, that the husbands are involved with adults, but the women are involved only with small children (Bernard, *op. cit.*, p. 154).

Bernard asks, "Is it possible that many women are 'happily married' *because* they have poor mental health?" (Bernard, *op. cit.*, p. 157). She cites a study by Johnson and Terman in 1935, which noted that happily married women were, among other things, docile rather than aggressive, indecisive, cautious rather than daring, and not very self-sufficient. She concludes with the rhetorical question, "Could it be that marriage itself is 'sick'?" (Bernard, *op. cit.*, p. 158).

A NEW ORDER

There are more radical feminists than Bernard who would restructure society into altogether different groupings. For Phyllis Chesler,

> the only acceptable groups are those that, unlike the family, can function as places of authentic responsibility and joy; as ways of supporting our deepest cravings for individual liberty, security, achievement, and love. Groups...which in any way kill the individual spirit...which enforce conformity, mediocrity, and conservatism - *for any reason*...such groupings are "male" and "female" rather than human groupings. (Chesler, 1973, p. 282)

Where does this all lead? Perhaps the following statement gives some indication:

> Recognition of the validity of the lesbian life style and acceptance of lesbian activism in women's liberation is crucial to the women's movement's ultimate goal - a new, harmonious, cooperative, non-authoritarian society in which men and women are free to be themselves. (Abbot and Love, in Gornick and Moran, 1972, p. 621)

In other words, the new society would be able to manage all its pleasures and turn-ons without men. Lest one think that this is a new twist to the social structure, long ago such practices seemed to abound. In the Biblical admonition to keep away from the abominations of Egypt and Canaan, the observation is made; "and what did they (in Egypt and Canaan) do? The man would marry a man and the woman would marry a woman" (Sifra, *Leviticus*, 18:3). For Juliet Mitchell, the ultimate goal is the overthrow of the patriarchy, or the next sequel to the overthrow of capitalism (Mitchell, 1974).

The paranoid would very likely label Women's Liberation as a communist plot. Gilder is certainly not off the mark when he observes that the Women's Liberation Movement is designed to emancipate us from "the very institution that is most indispensible to overcoming our present social crisis: the family" (Gilder, *op. cit.*, p. 6).

Women's Liberation has caused a counter reaction, admittedly not as massive, but nevertheless real — the movement of Men's Liberation. Jack Nichols contends that

A saner society will flower when men liberate themselves from contrived, socially fabricated prohibitions, cultural straitjackets, and mental stereotypes that control and inhibit behavior through arbitrary definitions of what it means to be a man. (Nichols, 1975, p. 317)

Nichols actually blames men for being the cause of women being "entrusted" with the upbringing of children. Equality of the sexes means that the worst features of the nuclear family unit need to be removed. Nichols suggests not that we discourage nuclear families, but rather that the relationships between parents and their children become "voluntary rather than obligatory" (ibid., p. 254). Nichols claims that children must be given their own autonomy. They must be free from institutionalized life-styles and be allowed to develop their own images (ibid., pp. 260-261).

The cycle is complete — from Women's Liberation to Men's Liberation to Children's Liberation, all under the amorphous guise of becoming oneself.

The radical wing of Women's Liberation would like to see an obliteration, even biologically, of the differences between man and woman. "Science must be used to either release women from biological reproduction — or to allow men to experience the process also" (Chesler, op. cit., p. 299). The movement would destroy the differences and create one class of human beings; no more men and women, only persons.

Recently, it has been found that many expectant fathers experience nausea, dizziness, heartburn, headache, abdominal cramps, etc., during their wives' pregnancies, all of which "mysteriously" disappear after the wife's delivery. But none of these fathers has ever actually had a baby.

Ironically, the Talmud reports a situation in which a sexual juxtaposition took place. It relates the story of a man whose wife had just died and who could not afford paying what was necessary to nurse his young child. Miraculously he grew womanly breasts and was able to feed his child (*Shabbat*, 53b).

One Talmudic reaction to this was of open admiration for the greatness of this individual because such a miracle had been wrought for him. Another reaction was the opposite — how lowly an individual he must have been that the order of creation was changed on his account! Rashi, in a comment which neutralizes any male chauvinism, explains that the lowliness was because he did not merit that a means for earning money was opened for him.

It is important to note that even the view which glorifies this individual does so because it was a miracle wrought for him. Obviously the same admiration would not obtain if an individual were to medically change biological states.

It is an ironic twist that the Women's Liberation movement, which began by establishing a separate category of people called women, should go full circle and desire a social state in which there are no women. It would be very hard to duplicate such an expression of male chauvinism.

Obliterating all sex differences is a more extreme extension of the Freudian notion that woman is essentially a castrated male. Clara M. Thompson is correct in denouncing this view and in insisting that woman's identity is a positive reality (Thompson, 1971, p. 41).

As Gilder points out, cross-cultural studies indicate that males almost everywhere show greater sexual aggressiveness, compulsiveness, lack of selectivity, and are more prone to shallow and indiscriminate erotic activity (Gilder, *op.cit.*, p. 22). Thankfully, women are different.

The idea of open marriage with its recommendation of total juxtaposition of roles between husband and wife, short of reproduction, is seen by Gilder as

> an attempt to reduce women to the condition of men, abjectly dependent on external performance and achievement. It is an attempt to convert the rich dimensions of female eroticism into the short circuits of tension and release

to which the male without marriage is assigned. (Gilder, *op.cit.*, p. 62)

DIFFERENTNESS

A more moderate view is proposed by Leon Salzman who contends that:

> One sex is neither superior nor inferior to another: they are each different to the extent that they serve different biological roles. Otherwise they are alike; both want and need security, status, prestige, and acceptance; and both are capable of envy, greed, hostility, and masochism to the extent that their needs are frustrated. (Salzman, in Miller, 1973, p. 220)

More affirmative on the differences between men and women is Erik Erikson. He conducted experiments with boys and girls, aged ten to twelve, giving them various toys and asking them to create themes. In two-thirds of the 150 boys and two-thirds of the 150 girls, it was found that "the girls emphasized *inner* and the boys *outer* space" (Erikson, in Strouse, 1974, P. 298). Inner space, of course, refers to the home environment and outer space to the outside world.

Admittedly, these findings by Erikson must be tempered with the caution that often a person's self-image is a function of what is expected by others.

More militant is Julia Sherman, who argues that the idea of equality of men and women in the sense of sameness, not only equality of opportunity and equality of value, is a myth. Men and women, she says, are fundamentally different, as is evidenced by the many studies that she cites in this regard. Sherman expresses surprise that sex differences in development have been ignored in educational planning. She recommends more research on female functioning, pregnancy, childbirth, and child rearing and that individualized instruction take place for boys and girls (Sherman, 1971, p. 245).

REUVEN P. BULKA

Even accepting Sherman's views, one must be careful not to stereotype, because stereotyping does not tell the whole story. For example,

> It may be true that women are more emotional than men in romance, but they are less so in air raids. Their protective instinct for those they love is actually a shield against the nerve-shattering effects of warfare noises. They perform the job in hand with calmer deliberation than men. (Long, in Montagu, 1971, p. 96)

Stereotyping aside, the differences between men and women appear to be more than just biological or sociological. As Gilder contends, "There are no human beings; there are just men and women, and when they deny their divergent sexuality, they reject the deepest sources of identity and love. They commit sexual suicide" (Gilder, *op.cit.*, p. 46).

PRIORITIES AND ATTITUDES

Many aspects of the Women's Liberation Movement call for some comment. First, there seems to be a case of misplaced priorities at work. Dr. Spock tells of a conversation he had with one of his students who said she would be bored with child-rearing at home, but not with the agonizing and enervating task of child psychiatry because "the psychiatrist is trying to *accomplish* something" (Spock, 1971, p. 54).

The movement seems to have put many of its eggs in the career basket. But if career should be defined as the chief source of freedom and fulfillment, the psychological affect would be to doom most women to feelings of failure and inadequacy (Gilder, *op.cit.*, p. 7).

Montagu observes that:

> In our materialistic age, because we have placed far less value upon the qualities for being human than we have upon those for accomplishment in the arts, sciences, and technologies, our values have become confused, undeveloped, and we have almost forgotten what the true ones are. Surely the

110

most valuable quality in any human being is his capacity for being loving and cooperative. (Montagu, *op.cit.*, p. 164)

And as Gilder points out,

The woman assumes charge of what may be described as the domestic values of the community; its moral, aesthetic, religious, nurturant, social, and sexual concerns. In these values consist the ultimate goals of human life: all those matters that we consider of such supreme importance that we do not ascribe a financial worth to them. (Gilder, *op.cit.*, p. 259)

It may be true that the materialism of capitalistic society is the enemy, but there must be alternatives other than destroying that society en toto.

Another problem in the movement is the appearance of a self-centered approach. In Chesler's words, "Women must try to convert the singleminded ruthlessness with which they yearn for, serve, and protect a mate or biological child into the 'ruthlessness' of self-preservation and self-development" (Chesler, *op.cit.*, p. 301). In the ambience of this approach, women are urged to *"Adopt the attitude that you are not trying to have an orgasm with your partner to please him but to please yourself"* (Baer, 1976, p. 236).

Not surprisingly, with this attitude of "what's in it for me," women do not heartily accept the role of enabler, and this apparently applies also to Jewish women. As Saul Berman points out, "It is becoming increasingly difficult for Jewish women to accept the idea that their own religious potential is exhausted in enabling their husbands and children to fulfill *mitzvot*" (Berman, 1973, p. 9).

This raises the question of the famous Talmudic observation that women earn their merit by bringing their children to the synagogue to learn Scripture, enabling their husbands to frequent the Bet Hamidrash to learn Mishnah, and waiting for their husbands to return from the Bet Hamidrash (*Berakhot*, 17a). Perhaps what is objectionable in this enabling process is not the enabling itself, for as the Talmud says, "One who causes another to do good is greater than the doer" (*Baba Batra*, 9a). What is unwelcome is the chauvinism which is bred into the male who expects and even

REUVEN P. BULKA

demands this of his wife. Here again, there is a suspicion that there has been some capitulation to materialistic, career-oriented values. Blu Greenberg points out that "we must not coerce all women into a new restrictive mold - that which excludes enablers" (Greenberg, in Koltun, 1976, p. 187).

Judaism is community-based rather than individually oriented, and God-centered rather than identity-centered. Greenberg observes that "charity and giving of oneself to others are being undercut in the fight for self-actualization...Those who find satisfaction in giving of themselves to others should be praised, not scorned" (ibid., p. 190).

There is a psychological aspect of this approach that must be further taken into account; the fact that self-actualization is self-defeating and is, in fact, a bottomless pit. As Frankl points out;

Human existence is essentially self-transcendence rather than self-actualization. Self-actualization is not a possible aim at all, for the simple reason that the more a man would strive for it, the more he would miss it. For only to the extent to which man commits himself to the fulfillment of his life's meaning, to this extent he also actualizes himself. (Frankl, 1968, p. 175)

The bottomless pit of self-actualization is a vital consideration in any approach to the woman's role. Emphasis on self-gratification is likely to lead to frustration and more radical desires, or to the desperate hope that somewhere in elusive space fulfillment will be found. It is possible that the radical wing of the movement, which emphasizes the fulfillment of the self, is just a few steps ahead of where the moderate wing eventually will be forced. The notion of fulfilling the other has already been shown to be not only philosophically more luadable, but clinically more functional. This must be carefully taken into account in the present circumstances.

JUDAISM AND FEMINISM

In considering the relevance of Women's Liberation to Judaism, it must be appreciated that Jewish feminism is related to feminism in general. Judith Plaskow observes that woman's sense of exclusion "arises partly from the fact that everything in our written tradition comes from the hands of men. The *halakhah*, most obviously, is the product of many generations of men. The same is true of the *aggadah*. The bible was written by men" (Plaskow, in Koltun, 1975, p.4). Was there, indeed, a masculine plot deriving from God to subjugate the female?

Orthodox Jewish feminists are, according to Anne Lapidus Lerner, a disturbing element, "for they will not indefinitely be satisfied to remain in a passive role in segregated sections of the synagogue" (Lerner, 1977, p. 16). There is indeed a unique problem concerning Orthodox Jewish feminists. Eliezer Berkovits justly questions whether all the explications of what is possible within the law have already been given (Berkovits, 1976, p. 117). And, as Miriam Feldman contends,

> if there is room to permit certain practices without injuring the integrity of *Halakhah*, it should be seriously considered. This does not imply the compromise of Torah values. On the contrary, it would vigorously demonstrate the belief that the Torah can weather the pressing problems of today, as it has in the past, with courage and resiliency. (Feldman, 1976 - 1977, p. 21)

The question of what is possible within the *halakhah* must be complemented with the equally valid question of what is desirable for the state of Jewish life and of society. That is a more difficult and perhaps even more crucial question in formulating a Jewish approach.

Within the realm of normative practice, a number of individuals have come up with their own rituals. One couple has designed a ritual for the birth of a daughter to include *Sheva Berakhot* as in a wedding, with one of the blessings being, curiously, the blessing one recites upon seeing a rainbow. Also, there is a redeeming of the first born daughter (Leifer and Leifer, in Koltun, 1975, pp. 21-30). Another contribution is a new unique form of *Bat Mitzvah* where instead of a *tallit*, the girls make headbands with scriptural verses of their own choosing inscribed on them (Koller-Fox, in Koltun, 1975, pp. 40-41).

Some have introduced a new, and in their view, more balanced *ketubah* (marriage contract) (Liefer, in Koltun, 1975, pp. 50-61). Another proposed suggestion is that *Rosh Hodesh* become a woman's holiday, even though it already is a woman's holiday. The new suggestion is that it should be accompanied by special rituals and prayers (Agus, in Koltun, 1975, pp. 84-93). In this same spirit, one feminist has performed radical surgery to make a Jewish woman's *haggadah*. Her first task was to make God "Ruler of the universe" instead of "King" (Zuckoff, in Koltun, 1975, p. 95). Feminists probably do not realize that long ago Jews of Galicia had taken any sexist implications out of the reference to God, whom they addressed as *Hakudoish Burich He*. (*He* is the particular twist of the Jews of Galicia for *Hu*. *Hu* is masculine and *He* is feminine, or *Hu* is He and *He* is She).

A more radical proposal is offered by Mary Gendler. She suggests two new rituals. The first is a ritual rupturing of the hymen, (or should it be hyperson), soon after birth. The operation should, of course, be performed by a woman. The second suggestion, if the girl wishes, is a special blessing and perhaps celebration upon the occasion of her menstruation, which, assuredly, would have to be renamed womenstruation (Gendler, 1974-75, p. 73).

Gendler's suggested new ritual is curiously missing from the otherwise beefy section on new rituals in the book edited by Koltun. Perhaps Koltun was embarrassed to include it, but this obviously gives an indication of where the trend might go, uncomfortable as it might be. Radicalism is not restricted to secular norms!

Blu Greenberg suggests, on the more moderate scale, that the operating principle, "one who is involved in fulfilling a precept is exempt from fulfilling other precepts" (Talmud, *Sukkah*, 25a) be employed to excuse women from mitzvot during child-rearing years (Greenberg, in Koltun, 1976 p.182). At other times, of course, if this is not operative, women would not be excused. In Greenberg's view, we must even have women *halakhic* authorities or *poskim* (ibid., p. 173). Again the question here is not merely one of *halakhic* propriety, but how to deal responsibily within the *halakhah* with the ultimate societal implications of Women's Liberation.

WOMEN AND COMMANDMENT

It has been contended that "The most formidable barrier to change and to the acceptance of women as authority figures and as the equals of men lies in the psychological rather than the halakhic realm" (Hyman, in Koltun, 1976, p. 109).

The observation, even if true, does not lessen the problem. *Halakhah* itself must be psychologically responsible. Indeed, a very strong case can be made for the fact that *halakhah* is fomulated on an authoratative understanding of the true nature of men and women, the means through which their characters can be molded and their best traits elicited. In fact, in espousing belief in the Divine origin of the Torah, it is hardly possible to assume anything less. Bandwagonning, even within the domain of *halakhah* but outside the psychological realm, is an approach which must be considered suspect. It might alleviate a momentary crisis, but in the end may set into motion a harmful chain of events. Perhaps a more militant approach to the entire question of Women's Liberation should be pondered, an approach in which the uniqueness of women is positively espoused and elicited.

Berman suggests that women's exception from commandments associated with time (Talmud, *Berakhot*, 20b) is "to assure that no legal obligation would interfere with the selection by Jewish women of a role which was centered almost exclusively in the home" (Berman, *op.cit.*, p. 17).

One could go a step further and theorize that the differences were also intended to establish the radical otherness of male and female in that though they are alike in what they could not do, they were different in what they had to do. This specific exemptive quality within the *halakhah*, which is a more positive affirmation of the uniqueness of the sexes than the famous commandment, "A man's implements should not be on a woman, and a man shall not wear a woman's garment, for everyone who does these things is an abomination of God, your God" (*Deuteronomy*, 22:5), serves to program what *halakhah* obviously considered a healthy reality.

The healthy reality is perhaps best illustrated through the remarks made by Berman. He says,

> To suggest that women don't really *need* positive symbolic *mitzvot* because their souls are already more attuned to the Divine, would be an unbearable insult to men; unless it were understood, as it indeed is, that the suggestion is not really to be taken seriously but is intended solely to placate women. Could we really believe that after granting women this especially religiously attuned nature, God would entrust to men - with their inferior souls - the subsequent unfolding of His will for man as expressed in the *Halakhah*?" (Berman, *op.cit.*, p. 9)

The answer to Berman's question may very well be a resounding "yes." After all, did not Rav declare that "The precepts were given to Israel for the purpose of shaping humankind" (*Midrash Rabbah*, Genesis 44:1, and *Midrash Rabbah*, Leviticus 13:3). Obviously, if men were given more precepts than women, it is because they are in need of more shaping, because women are in better shape than they are. If the Divine will is towards bringing humankind to a specific level of spiritual excellence, then the fact that men have more commandments merely indicates that they need it in order to get there. It is possible, even logical, to take seriously the fact that women do not need positive symbolic mitzvot. It is not to placate women, nor is it an unbearable insult to men as much as it is a bearable challenge.

The famous Tamudic statement, "One who is commanded and fulfills is greater than one who is not commanded and fulfills" (*Kiddushin*, 31a) takes on added meaning. Since the commandments were given to uplift and bring the individual to a more exalted level, its utimate utility is achieved more for those to whom the commandment is addressed, rather than those for whom the commandment was not considered necessary; i.e., those who are fulfilling the command-plateau which *halakhah* perceived they had already reached.

WOMEN'S ESSENTIALITY

The notion of male inferiority, honestly projected, must be countered with the positive projection of woman's greatness. Byron said;

Man's love is of man's life a thing apart,
'Tis woman's whole existence.

Montagu asserts that *"It is the function of women to teach men how to be human"* (Montagu, *op.cit.*, p. 159). True humaness, in Montagu's concept, involves true love. Montagu claims that

True love is self-denying, so suffused with humility that those who exhibit it are not likely to dwell upon its meaning. Woman knows what true love is; let her not be tempted from her knowledge by the false idols that man has created for her to worship. Woman must stand firm and be true to her own inner nature; to yield to the prevailing false conceptions of love, of unloving love, is to abdicate her great evolutionary mission to keep human beings true to themselves...to help them to realize their potentialities for being loving and co-operative. Were woman to fail in this task, all hope for the future of humanity would depart form the world. (Montagu, ibid., p. 216)

Gilder echoes Montagu when he says that "there is no way that women can escape their supreme responibilities in civilization itself" (Gilder, *op.cit.*, p. 264).

Gilder is even more assertive concerning the importance of the family. He believes that the family is the "only agency which can induce truly profound and enduring changes in its members" (ibid, p. 77). Within the family there are essential roles for both man and woman. Gilder claims that the delicate balance between inner space and outer space is not only social reality, but healthy reality. Women are basically superior and integral to the family. Men cannot be expected to remain as integral parts of the family if their roles are obviously inferior to women, and they may even demand open subordination. In the trade-off, the husband must at least be the principal provider. In a matriarchy, the husband does not even do this and, having no tie to the family, will almost always leave (ibid., p. 113).

In Gilder's words:

the woman's place *is* in the home, and she does her best when she can get the man there too. That, she cannot easily do alone. The society has to provide a role for him, usually as provider, that connects him to the family in a masculine way. But if social conditions are right, the woman can induce the man to submit most human activity to the domestic values of civilization. (ibid., p. 263)

Within the family, child-rearing is one of the most vital staples. A society which places a great emphasis on child-rearing is likely to be generous and cooperative. There is no evidence from cross-cultural studies that roles can be switched back and forth (ibid., p. 59). This view is echoed by Rosemary Friedman, who claims that "though men may undertake, they can never succeed in, fulfilling the function of a woman as maker of a home" (Friedman, in Longworth, 1966, p. 135).

It is useful to point out that many of the problems which Women's Liberation has so successfully brought into sharper focus are linked not only to an over-materialistic emphasis, but also to the nuclear family structure, which Philippe Aries calls a "prison of love." It is important not only to glorify the family and emphasize that women are unique and vital to civilization, but also to broaden the family structure beyond its present nuclear state so that inter-relationships are more fluid and shared by more people, rather than burdened by the frustrations born of privacy and exclusivity.

The male population must approach the Women's Liberation situation with humility. They must bear in mind that in the future the woman's voice will be the more primary one, as Rabbi Schneur Zalman points out in explaining the verse "A virtuous woman is her husband's crown..." (*Proverbs*, 12:4). In the future Messianic time, the majesty of woman will no longer be hidden and will be the crown clearly visible on the head of man. When, in the seven blessings under the *huppah*, we pray for the time that the voice of the Kallah will be heard, and conclude the blessing with

"Who makes the groom to rejoice with the bride," this indicates that the voice of the bride in future time will be the main one (Seder Tefilot Mikal haShanah, 1965, pp. 276-277).

Rabbi Schneur Zalman's observation is consistent with the view here proposed that the abundance of *mitzvot* directed to men are not an indication of superiority, and, in fact, actually indicates the reverse. This world is merely a perparation for the time that woman's crown will actually be able to fit on the man's head; that is, when man will be deserving of such majesty as being the secondary beneficiary of the primary majesty of women.

FUTURE AGENDA

To project honestly the essential place of women in civilization and to defend militantly their unique role not only as necessary for the survival of Judaism, but of society itself, demands humility. It also demands the capacity to weather the present storm in the honest conviction that an unpopular stand may, nevertheless, be the correct one.

Margaret Mead's findings in anthropological studies were that women are most content not when granted power and influence, but when the female role of wife and mother is exalted (Mead, 1968, p. 110). At stake are not only woman's contentedness, but the integrity and stability of society in general and Jewish life in particular. A non-apologetic, affirmative stance to women is vital.

There are obvious and subtle ways in which this stance can be incorporated. Perhaps Rabbis today are paying the price for egocentrically stressing the importance of attending *shul* instead of emphasizing the Jewish home. Perhaps, too, in deciding who should be honoured by the community, attention should be given not to those who have been enabled, but to the enablers, those who in the Talmudic view are greater than the doers. The sincerity with which this is approached may convince women that man's conception of woman's importance is not merely apologetic, but is honestly felt and meant; not demanded, but appreciated.

One Jewish feminist claims that "the challenge of feminism, if answered, can only strengthen Judaism" (Hyman, *op.cit.*, p. 112).

119

This observation may be correct, but the answer might not be the expected one.

From a *halakhic*, psychological, and societal view, the Jewish answer may very well be: "To feminism, no; to women in their full uniqueness and authenticity, absolutely yes!"

CHAPTER 8

DIVORCE: THE PROBLEM AND THE CHALLENGE

It is common knowledge that divorce rates have risen steadily, if not spectacularly, in North America. The Jewish community has not escaped unscathed from this trend. Added to the statistical separations are the many "would be" divorces that never reach the final break, either because of religious inhibition or social stigma. Frequently, these cases can be more frustrating and damaging than actual divorces.

Unhappiness in a growing number of Jewish households is a cause of real concern. Why is it happening and what can be done about it? It is important that this situation be brought into the open and discussed seriously with a view toward reversing this trend.

What follows is not the result of broad surveys or intensive research. Rather, it is the quasi-objective views of one man. My purpose is not to throw stones or cast blame, but rather to initiate discussion and effective action.

REUVEN P. BULKA

CHARACTER DEFICIENCY

Marriage is the union of two individuals who, if they are of good character, should be able to live with each other. In cases where marraige fails, one or both of the partners has a deficient personality. What is called marriage breakdown is really a condition of retarded personality development coming to the fore. This retarded development leads to a distorted set of values and an inability to interact on a human level with people.

Huxley once said that "If individuality has no play, society does not advance; if individuality breaks out of all bounds, society perishes." The same dialectic is true of human development. It is best expressed in the famous words of Hillel, "If I am not for myself, who will be for me? And if I am for myself only, what am I?..." (Talmud, *Avot*, 1:14). To be self-effacing to the point of neglect is irresponsible; to be self-indulgent to the point of obliviousness to the other person is irresponsive. The person who best relates to other people is one who has taken care of individual needs, who has a well defined and developed sense of self and a sense of responsibility, with a realistic and honest appreciation of his/her role in life. The honest confrontation with one's self leads towards a healthy outer-directedness, or towards a concern with causes and for people. In short, the classic I-thou relationship between people demands an "I" to relate to a thou, but the real "I" will intentionally gravitate to a thou; not to fulfill a need but to share a self. The true relationship with another person emanates from self-transcendence rather than from self-actualization.

Sharing of the self with another, in the classical sense, is expressed in marital union. Maimonides, in his *Guide for the Perplexed* (Part 3, Chapter 49), suggests that the female relatives whom a man may not marry share one common ingredient - they are constantly with him in the house and arranging a marriage would be a relatively easy task. Maimonides also roundly condemns the union of root and branch and sees this as part of the reason for the prohibited consanguineous unions.

These two factors, the constant togetherness and the root-branch idea, point to a vital factor in any marriage. The respective spouses are obliged to marry people who are "strangers," people who can be called "other." Sticking to one's own confines is seen as abhorrent. This stems from the reality that such a union involves not an extension of self, but a turning in of the self, a shriveling up, or recoiling into a comfortable shell. It reinforces a self-centeredness that is the very antithesis of healthy human interaction.

Self-centeredness manifested in a form of hyper-reflection on the self is considered to be one of the prime causes of impotence and frigidity between couples. Whether it stems from a strong desire to be able to perform or an excessive drive for self-satisfaction, it results in increasing difficulty and frustration and, eventually, in an inability to communicate sexually with the partner. This has been recognized by the philosophically oriented psychologies such as Logotherapy as well as by sex therapists such as Masters and Johnson. Masters and Johnson use a technique closely resembling Logotheraphy's de-reflection to get the partners' minds off ultimate expression and to concentrate on each partner as a person. The best means of attaining the pleasure of marital union is by not intending it, but by letting it flow as the natural expression of a love relationship. Happiness, instead of being pursued, should ensue.

MATURE SHARING

It is instructive to use the sexual link as a paradigm for the viability of a marriage. Sex is the language of marriage. It is the distinct form of marital communication. The problem of hyper-reflection on the self which causes breakdowns in sexual communication is also at work in verbal communication. Paradoxically, when each partner is primarily concerned not with the self but with the other person, both the functional and spiritual aspects of the union are enhanced. The concept of extending the self toward the other is thus conceived, at once, as a philosophical and functional truth.

The self which extends toward the other, in the marital context, should be a mature self. Through growth and commitment, the mature self assumes responsibility for personal welfare. In the words of the Talmud, "a man should build a house, plant a vineyard, and then marry a woman" (*Sotah*, 44a).

Maimonides, in an extraordinary vignette, states that it is the way of fools first to marry and then to build a house and find a profession (Mishnah Torah, Laws of Tendencies [De'ot], 5:11). Before a person has established inner stability and peace, symbolized by the building of a home, and before having planted a vineyard, that is, before having placed himself on a firm financial footing, it is premature, even foolish, to marry. If the marriage itself is expected to create the financial and emotional stability that is missing prior to marriage, then the marriage is surely in trouble. Marriage, ideally, is the union of two complete people, who unite not to fulfill needs or satisfy drives, but to exercise mutual growth through reciprocal concern for each other. The ideal of immersion in the other can hardly be realized when each, or even one, still has unresolved problems or basic character deficiencies. In such cases, the wedlock is not one of true love, but, instead, an alliance for need gratification. It is caused and dependent rather than spontaneous and independent. Eventually "All love that depends on a cause will cease once the cause is no longer there, but that love which is not dependent on a cause will never cease" (Talmud, *Avot*, 5:16).

If it is stated that "Any man who has no wife is no proper man" (Talmud, *Yevamot*, 63a), this does not imply that man must marry at any cost. Rather, reaching maturity and self-sufficiency is only the first step in human endeavour. The next step is to extend the mature self toward another. The person who thinks that manhood is achieved through being independent and aloof is, in the words of the Talmud, no proper man. In all instances, true maturity is achieved via human dialogue, not in its absence.

The inability to share, to give of oneself, whether emanating from immaturity, or from the character deficiency best described as self-centeredness, is usually at work in marriage breakdowns. It is a personality flaw coming to the fore, albeit with sometimes tragic consequences. It is crucial at this juncture to study some possible ways of tackling the problem at the root.

THE PROBLEM

In trying to pinpoint the genesis of a problem in human development, it is first necessary to look at the home. If the home is to claim priority in importance as a Jewish institution, it must

124

also be prepared to shoulder blame for not having lived up to its billing.

What in the home is at fault? Perhaps we must point to parents without adequate time for their children. Possibly, it is the lack of a proper educational model for children to emulate in the home. If kindness, understanding, and empathy are not lived, they can hardly be transmitted. If children are taught to fend for themselves in a dog-eat-dog world, they may become self-sufficient, which is delightful for the parents, but a disaster for the children. They enter the adult world with caution, if not suspicion, and a protective, self-indulgent attitude.

If the problem is one of proper educational models, a practical problem arises. It might be simple to point out the lack of models to the parent generation, but it is another matter to help an entire generation of parents out of the rut. No doubt, every parent can do much in individual situations, but a grass roots approach at this stage, while not to be discounted, is not the full answer.

The school, of course, is the sphere where the main education takes place. It is very unlikely that adequate human values can be taught in a public school system. These school systems work within a neutralistic framework, exercising care not to offend any particular group. When it is reported that divorce problems are increasing among graduates of Yeshiva, the concern must be great. *Yeshivot*, even day schools and Hebrew High Schools, are supposedly centers for value transmission. The presence of human development problems among graduates of these institutions suggests something might be missing in the education given to the students.

Again, this is not to blame *Yeshivot*. It is to suggest that *Yeshivot*, being aware of the problems of the day, should react accordingly and investigate where they can improve. *Yeshivot*, potentially, can have a great influence on the course of Jewish life in the next few decades. As institutions, they have the capacity to make adjustments with far-reaching implications. The program they embark upon reaches so many individual students and the example offered by the teachers subtly influences so many in their ambience.

REUVEN P. BULKA

CURRICULUM PRIORITY

Yeshivot and other Jewish education systems place great emphasis on learning and knowledge. Very little stress is placed on character development. Values are discussed and many lectures deal with areas of concern such as charity, kindness, responsibility, etc. To graduate one may be required to know about them, but not necessarily to exhibit these virtues in real life.

One Talmudic view held that "Any student whose inner character does not correspond to his exterior may not enter the house of study" (*Berakhot*, 23a). This view did not prevail in the long run, as the ideal of trying to shape character in the house of study was of greater importance. This is what houses of study are for, as indeed the precepts of the Torah were given so that individuals might be refined by them (*Midrash Rabbah*, Genesis, 44:1). Still, the Talmud maintained that "Any scholar whose inner character is not consistent with his exterior is no scholar" (*Yoma*, 72b); is even called abominable.

This is in the realm of practical judgement. On a philosophical level, concerning the question whether learning or good deeds are more important, the consensual decision is "Study is greater, for it leads to action" (Talmud, *Kiddushin*, 40b). Learning which is disassociated from action is not true learning, as scholarship bereft of good character and good deeds is not true scholarship. If our schools are obliged to produce real scholars, this can only be done, philosophically and realistically, by producing true human beings of noble, caring character.

As initial suggestions to this end, I propose the following: (1) Every Yeshiva and Jewish school should embark on a program of character development along Torah lines that would be part of the cirriculum; (2) no student should be allowed to graduate from the Judaic section of the school who does not meet specific standards of character, the same as with failing grades; (3) the hiring of Rabbis, teachers, and administrative staff should be done with extra stress on finding outstanding educational models of sharing; caring personalities who live Judaism as much and as well as they teach it. They can influence by deed as well as by word.

These proposals may seem quite simple, yet the re-orientation needed to achieve these aims is no easy matter. It will take courage, perseverance, and delicate wisdom. The fruits of this reorientation will hopefully be students who are masters of human behaviour, and who can enter the marriage arena with all the ingredients that are required in healthy human interaction.

A match of spouses is known as a *shidukh*. Rabbi Moshe Isserless identifies this with the word *menuhah*, contentedness (Shulhan Arukh, Yoreh Deah, 228:43). No one today can be content with the state that many *shidukhim* find themselves. Yet Jews throughout history have been able to react positively to crisis and on countless occasions have been able to transmute potential tragedy into human triumph. If Jews today can restore the connotation of contentedness to the marital sphere, it will rank as a singular achievement of the will.

The problem is obvious; the need for action, imperative.

SECTION THREE

THE COMMUNITY
CHAPTER 9

TOWARDS A PSYCHOLOGICALLY SOUND JUDAISM

Psychotherapy was born, nurtured and developed with the sincere desire to correct what were perceived to be aberrations from the spectrum of "normal" behaviour. In the process, the thinking which went along with the therapy was obviously coloured by the subject matter at hand - people with differing degrees of disturbances. Much has thus been affected by what has been labelled as the "sick model."

The philosophical component within therapy has become a subject of concern. It is obvious that every therapy is underlined by a philosophy, although this philosophy is often quite subtle. In Frankl's words, "Every school of psychology has a concept of man, although this concept is not always held consciously" (1967, p. xvi). The potency of a philosophy relative to the clinic has been aptly spelled out by Allport, who asked rhetorically, "May not (sometimes at least) an acquired world-outlook constitute the central motive of a life and, if it is disordered, the ultimate therapeutic problem?" (1961, p. 97).

Albee, in what may turn out to be a prophetic statement, proposes the possibilty that:

the next large group to appear on the intervention scene will be the applied philosophers. Conditions seem right for the emergence of a philosophical therapy.... The problems of a

131

great many people who are seeing psychotherapists are concerned with a search for the meaning of existence, for purpose, identity. It seems probable that a well-trained PhD in philosophy, particularly if the philosopher is well-grounded in logic, ethics, and existential phenomenology, is well prepared to become a psychotherapist. I hope this development comes soon, because I believe that large numbers of clinical philosophers would be powerful allies for psychology in attempting to throw off the domination of the sickness (or defect) model. (1975, p. 1157)

One area in which the defect model seems to have had a significant impact concerns the role of religion in human development. Most people would conclude that psychotherapy, from its very origins, had a negative attitude to religion. It would be more correct to say that the negativity was directed not at religion per se, but at that religion which was observed to have caused complications in the arena of human expression. This chapter proposes to examine the view that religion may have a healthy role to play in psychotherapy, and to suggest the specific applicability of this view to Judaism.

MEETING GROUND

Science usually deals with the observable, the testable and the measurable. Religion deals with that which cannot be observed - God, heaven, hell, soul, immortality, etc. A more specific branch of science - psychology, is concerned with health and function. Religion, on the other hand, is more concerned with purpose. Erich Fromm sees some overlap between the two, as the analyst is "concerned with the very same problems as philosophy and theology: the soul of man and its cure" (1950, p. 7). Overlap, however, does not necessarily imply common direction, but a correlation of purpose would be mandatory to effect such common direction.

Schleiermacher, for example, held that religion's primary focus was on dependence, establishing the individual's helplessness and thus total reliance on an orientation around God. Psychology, on the other hand, directs itself towards individual happiness, contentedness, and self-reliance, even independence.

Obviously, any rapprochement between psychology and religion must directly confront the fact that the two disciplines move in almost opposite directions.

Abraham Maslow has proposed that the frames of reference of science and religion should be fused. Science should be prepared to study values and religion should be exposed to scientific inquiry (1970). The strict religionist might see a risk in this, a risk that scientific study of values might lead to the rejection of these values. In my view there is very little to lose and perhaps much to gain by exposing religion to scientific inquiry.

Some findings by Frankl (1975) contain encouraging prospects for the religionist. For example, one study showed that a higher sense of purpose in life usually was associated with a less pronounced fear of death. Certain forms of narcotic addiction seem to be related to a lower score on purpose-in-life. Some studies have shown that alcoholics tend to feel that their existence is meaningless and without purpose. Therapeutically speaking, the eliciting of the meaning factor amongst narcotic addicts and juvenile delinquents is an approach which has the lowest recidivism rate by far when compared with other interventionist approaches (Frankl, 1975, pp. 99-103).

Values have been employed quite successfully in clinical situations and have, in many instances, stood up to the rigours of scientific examination. If we accept Frankl's definition of the human as a being in search of meaning and his definition of religion as man's search for ultimate meaning (c.f. Bulka, 1979, pp. 35-57), it is apparent that there is a common direction shared between science and religion, or more specifically, psychotherapy and religion.

Erich Fromm defines religion as *"any system of thought and action shared by a group which gives the individual a frame of orientation and an object of devotion"* (1950, p. 21). Fromm further declares (p. 25) that there is "no one without a religious need, a need to have a frame of orientation and an object of devotion." How this need is expressed is a matter of individual choice, but within Fromm's all-encompassing definition, animal worship, idolatry, nationalism, capitalism, or running after success are all forms of religious expression. The vital question is - which religious orientation is conducive to human growth?

Mowrer, in an anti-Freudian harangue (1961), claims that psychopathology "instead of stemming from unexpressed sex and hostility, comes rather from an outraged conscience and violated sense of human decency and responsibility" (p. 131). Although this may seem to be an overgeneralization, it is a useful observation which perhaps establishes some form of balance. We can therefore include repressed meaningfulness or repressed religiousness in the list of possible causes of psychopathology. The net result is that an authentically expressed quest for meaning or an authentically expressed religiousness is conducive to and expressive of desirable health.

INTERNAL STRIFE

Science or psychology are not the only expressions of an unfavourable verdict concerning religion. Religion itself has often rendered condemnatory judgments concerning itself. Jewish history is replete with instances of intense tension which often created schisms within the community itself. The Pharisee-Sadducee conflict, the rift between the early Christian sect and Judaism, the Hasid vs. Mitnaged controversy, and the Orthodox-Reform polarization are testimony to the difficulties in religious expression.

The common denominator in these historical confrontations is the matter of halakhah (law), or, as it is pejoratively called, legalism. In the Pharisee-Sadducee controversy, the normative Judaism espoused by the Pharisees was attacked by the Sadducees, who argued for a stricter and more constricting view which would not admit Rabbinic interpretation with its broad sensitivity to real life situations. In the other conflicts, normative Judaism was on the other side of the argument, that is, accused of excessive legalism, of placing law above everything else to the detriment of the community. The Hasidim, for example, would accuse their opponents of possessing a fear of sinning against the law instead of a fear of sinning against God. The harangues of the early Christians against the Pharisees and the rejection of the Rabbinic world-view by the early Reformers are well known.

In all three instances, the revolt against the norm was an attempt to escape from the shackles of an institution too tightly bound by adherence to the law. The attempts to break free from the perceived constricting atmosphere brought interesting results.

Early Christianity developed into a totally different, but full-fledged religion of its own, complete with its own set of legal norms which were, in many ways, more severe than Judaism. Hasidism developed to a point where its adherence to the halakhah is more Orthodox than the Orthodox. And Reform Judaism evolved a theology of its own which presently contains an expanding, though decidely different, code of laws, a reform halakhah, of sorts. In almost every age there is a dissatisfaction with the status quo, coupled with a resolve to do things better. This resolve often translates into a variation of the original theme, and not necessarily an improvement. Tradition, it appears, continually resurfaces as a magnetic attraction.

DEVIANCE IN RELIGION

There is empirical evidence that all is not right within religion. The apparent corruption of supposedly religious figures, the insensitivity of those from whom one would have expected empathy, the protection of vested interest in place of outer-directed concern, are examples. As Fromm put it,

It is easy to see that many who profess the belief in God are in their human attitude idol worshippers or men without faith, while some of the most ardent "atheists," devoting their lives to the betterment of mankind, to deeds of brotherliness and love, have exhibited faith and a profoundly religious attitude. (1950, p. 113)

But there is more varied empirical evidence. Derek Wright points out that in tests of honesty, those with religious upbringing are not distinguishable from those without (1971, p. 232). In tests measuring the religion factor relative to Kohlberg's stages of moral development, it was found that morality scores were inversely connected with religious expression. Atheists, in fact, scored highest on these tests (Stevens, Blank, & Poushinsky, 1977). This at once gives credence to Fromm's argument about the "religiousness" of atheists and the faithlessness of some religionists. It also compels us towards a more profound definition of religion together with some guidelines for authentic religious expression.

Allport, in his classic, *The Individual and His Religion* (1950), distinguished between mature and immature religion. Immature religion is concerned with magical thinking, self-justification and creature comfort. Mature religion is not a servant of drives and desires, but a master, tending to direct the person towards goals which go beyond self-interest (p. 72).

Having goals or ideals is vital in achieving what Allport calls "integration," the forging of mental units out of discordent impulses and aspiration. Allport sees this as psychology's chief contribution to mental health. At the same time, the religious interest, the most comprehensive, is seen as the best integrative agent (pp. 103-104). Maslow echoes this in his statement that not having core-religious experiences indicates a state of dissociation, reduction to the concrete, neuroticizing, not being sufficiently integrated (1970, p. 32).

In this orientation around outer-directed goals, one attempts to bridge the subject-object split through dynamic awareness, awareness which is clothed in the garb of existential anxiety. Hora sees this as the meeting point of psychotherapy and religion, since in this anxiety, we "are confronted with the task of helping man accept the 'human condition' and through genuine acceptance transcend his despair and separation from the world, thus reaching an authentic existence which is ontically integrated" (1962, p. 78).

HUMANE RELIGION

If Allport and Maslow espouse the concept of integration as effected by religion, Fromm hones in on the more humane elements implied by the concept of integration. He distinguishes between authoritarian and humanistic religion. Authoritarian religion demands surrender to a higher power. Obedience is the highest virtue. In this surrender, there is a trade-off, as one loses independence but gains protection. In sum, however, the person is the big loser. For in authoritarian religion, God becomes the possessor of all that belonged to the individual, including reason and love. The self is impoverished, as all virtue is concentrated in God. One becomes alienated from the self, with the only access to the self being through God.

Humanistic religion, in Fromm's view, is different. Such religion is characterized by love for the self and others - the one being a prerequisite for the other, reminiscent of the Biblical command to "love your neighbour as yourself" (*Leviticus*, 19:18). In humanistic religion, one feels integrated or at one with all. The aim of humanistic religion is to elicit one's strength in the prevailing mood of joy.

Fromm suggests what might possibly be employed as a litmus test for "legitimate" religion. If it contributes to the growth, strength, freedom, and happiness of the believers, it is the fruits of love. If it contributes to the constriction of human potentialities, to unhappiness and lack of productivity, it cannot be born of love.

This proposal should be mediated by a number of considerations. First, although Fromm seems to have little patience for dogmatic religion, which is more concerned with regulation than with empathy, it is vital to distinguish between dogma for dogma's sake and dogma as the basic structural framework within which human expression should operate. Second, placing such heavy emphasis on the element of self-realization is dangerous for the very reasons that Fromm would condemn aberrant religion - the worship of self-realization can itself become an idolatry.

The notion of happiness and joy should be placed in the context enunciated by John Stuart Mill. Happiness, Mill argued, can be found by focusing on something external, such as the happiness of others, the improvement of mankind or some other pursuit, actualized not as a means but as an ideal end. One should not focus on or treat happiness, but should commit one's self to causes outside of one's self. Mill went on to say that "This theory now becomes the basis of my philosophy of life" (quoted in Menninger, 1967, p. 407).

REUVEN P. BULKA

RIGHT ATMOSPHERE AND ORIENTATION

From a Judaic perspective, the psalmaic imperative - "Serve God with joy..." (*Psalms*, 100:2) may thus be proposed as a major thesis concerning religious expression. This, of course, can only work in the context of outer-directedness. Although psychology is normally concerned with the self, clinicians and thinkers are more and more adopting the self-transcending dynamic. Ellis speaks of commitment to something outside the self, such as people, things, or ideas around which life should be structured (1973, p. 160). Maslow avers that "basic human needs can be fulfilled *only* by and through other human beings" (1970, p. xii). Even Fromm makes mention of the concern with the meaning of life, with the fulfillment of the task which life sets. These views are most manifest in the thought and therapy of Viktor Frankl, who has structured his system around the notion of self-transcendence as an essential element in the human dynamic. Others speak about it; Frankl builds on it.

The emphasis on going beyond one's self as opposed to the Schleiermacherian conception of dependence should not be lost on the religious community. The notion of self-transcendence fits in quite well with Judaic philosophy. For example, the idea of "Let all your actions be for the sake of Heaven" (Talmud, *Avot*, 2:12), establishes an all embracing dynamic which is not only self-transcending, but also oriented around the transcendent. Here one finds psychology and religion going in the same direction, with religion going a bit further.

The self-transcending person is good by virtue of performing good deeds and orienting the activities of life around goodness. The self is affirmed, albeit tangentially. The all embracingness of "Let all your actions be for the sake of Heaven" has its counterpart in Maslow's impression that serious people of all kinds "tend to be able to 'religionize' *any* part of life, *any* day of the week, in *any* place" (1970, p. 31). Concomitantly, the sacred is "*in* the ordinary,....it is to be found in one's daily life, in one's neighbors, friends, and family, in one's backyard" (Maslow, 1970, p. x).

Compartmentalized goodness is not consistent with authentic religiousness. It should be noted that Maslow was an avowed atheist, yet his suggestions concerning authentic religiousness capture the dynamic flavour of what Judaism should be. The emphasis he places on sanctifying the every day echoes the famous Talmudic dictum, "when it is a choice between that which is regular and that which is not as regular, the regular has priority" (Talmud, *Berakhot*, 51b).

It may be surprising that an avowed atheist should espouse religious categories. Yet, Fromm did caution us that some atheists, in fact, display truly religious behaviour. Fromm's views should also serve to clarify the apparent distrust of religion by psychology. It is not a distrust of religion per se - it is a distrust of the abuse of religion. Incorporating the humane features of psychology into religion can serve to keep religion focused in the right direction. The fusion of the two seems to be best incorporated in the observation of Paul Pruyser, who stated that mental health should not be seen as homeostasis, but as a realization of values that are only achievable through the process of becoming, as opposed to merely being (1958).

There is an historical link betwen authentic Judaism and its espousal of outer directedness via the deed and its later affirmation in so many different colourations, be it Mill's philosophy, Pruyser's psychology, Ellis' clinical approach, or the thinking of Maslow, Fromm, and Frankl. The commandments within Judaism must be seen as means rather than ends in themselves (Bulka, 1973). So many basic categories exist within Judaism which, if implemented as proposed, would never allow commandments to become dogma. Such ideas as *lifnim meshurat hadin* - working within the boundaries of the law, (Talmud, *Berakhot*, 7a, 45b; *Ketuvot*, 97a; *Baba Kama* 99b, 100a; *Baba Mezia* 24b, 30b); *midot hasidut* - the way of the pious, (Talmud, *Shabbat* 120a; *Baba Mezia* 52b; *Hullin* 130b); *v'aseeta hayashar v'hatov* - doing that which is upright and good (*Deuteronomy*, 6:18; Talmud, *Baba Mezia* 16b, 108a; *Avodah Zarah* 25a); and *l'maan telech bderech tovin* - to walk in the way of good people (*Proverbs*, 2:20; Talmud, *Baba Mezia* 83a), are ample illustration that within Judaism, the law is conceived as a framework. It is the human being in individual uniqueness who gives meaningful expression within that framework.

The human investment in the Divine commandment is what gives the commandment its life. "Charity is rewarded only according to the kindness accompanying it" (Talmud, *Sukkah* 49b).

REUVEN P. BULKA

The charity is the obligation, or more precisely, the framework. The kindness is the human investment which gives it authenticity.

LAW AS MEANS

Isaiah long ago castigated the people because their fear of God was a "commandment of people learned by rote" (Isaiah, 29:13). The prophet condemns the programmed Jew, who is perfunctorily exact but has reduced the self to a lifeless person. This person does not respond to situations in the freedom and spontaneity of human conscience within Judaic guidelines. It is not in the law, but rather within and through the law that authentic Judaism is expressed. The law is the framework carefully constructed to elicit the highest level of one's social and spiritual essence. Lived for its own sake, the law is stultifying. Lived as the jumping off points for human expression, the law invests life with meaning.

The Shabbat, for example, contains an abundance of minute and exacting regulations. However, it is not fulfilled in merely adhering to these regulations, but rather in seeing these regulations as the guidelines within which true human expression is possible. By cutting one off from materially creative concerns, the law forces the individual into a higher dimension where the concerns are intellectual and spiritual. In another instance of exacting legislation, the laws of kashrut gain greatest viability when seen as the elicitor of humane feeling. This is one of the major themes in the legislation itself, but is often lost on the practitioners.

The classic story of Rabbi Israel Salanter illustrates the necessary humaneness that must emanate from adherence. As the Rabbi's students were preparing to bake the matzah for Passover, they asked for some last minute advice. Rabbi Salanter told them that when they prepare the ingredients they should be especially mindful of the poor lady who has to drag the water necessary for kneading the dough. He instructed his students to be especially sensitive to her and not to become oblivious or insensitive in their overzealousness.

INDIVIDUAL, FAMILY, COMMUNITY:
JUDEO -PSYCHOLOGICAL PERSPECTIVES

The Rabbi Salanter story is as depressing as it is exciting. It is an outstanding story, but its very outstandingness indicates that the humane ingredient within the legal framework is a rarity glorified through storytelling instead of being sanctified by practice.

The Bible instructed those who would go up to the altar in the following manner - "And not by steps shall you go up onto my altar, that your nakedness be not uncovered thereon" (*Exodus*, 20:23). The Mekhilta elicits a humane application from a seemingly transcendent regulation. It proposes the following: If Scripture was so scrupulous concerning stones, which have no thought processes to be mindful of their shame, how much more so must one be mindful of shaming one's friend, who has been created in God's image and possesses a sense of shame?

Even the most remote commandment is escalated into a human imperative. The ingredients are there for vitalizing Jewishness. It is a philosophical, theological, and, in the 20th century, psychological imperative to employ these ingredients.

Maslow believes that a person who sees the consequences of growth and regression would choose the consequence of growth and reject the consequence of regression. In a similar vein, the Bible, in offering a choice between life and good versus death and the bad (*Deuteronomy*, 30:15), recommends that one "choose life" (*ibid.*, 30:19), rather than recommending that one choose good. Life is the good, but the clear choice is not as much a moral choice as it is a growth choice. Life is the primary factor and good is that which emanates from life and feeds back into it. For Maslow and his colleagues, it is a psychological choice. For Jews and Judaism, it is a theological choice consistent with the aspirations of a self-transcending psychology. Clearly science and religion, and in the present context, psychology and Judaism, can not only complement each other, they can serve to bring one another into their own; to make manifest that which is latent and thus, to place religion in its proper place on the human agenda.

CHAPTER 10

CHARACTERISTICS OF RABBINIC LEADERSHIP - A PSYCHOLOGICAL VIEW

We live in a psychological society, as Martin Gross has argued (Gross, 1978). We seek simultaneously the psychological roots of past behaviour and the parameters by which to predict future behaviour for all segments of society.

The Jewish community in North America is definitely part of this so-called psychological society. We are at an interesting if not crucial stage in our development, inching towards maturity, understandably insecure because of our past and wary of our future. Though there are forces beyond our control which will help shape Judaism's future, there are other forces within our community which will play a large role in shaping the Judaism of the next decade. One of these forces is the Rabbinate. A healthy Rabbinate will contribute to a healthy Judaism; a disturbed, uncomfortable Rabbinate will contribute to an ambivalent Judaism. To analyze the state of the Rabbinate and its Rabbis thus is a most vital exercise.

REUVEN P. BULKA

One must begin with the individual Rabbi, and to understand the individual Rabbi one must focus on a multitude of
personal and interactional facets of Rabbinic life. This presentation
focuses on the following aspects of the Rabbi's function: (1) The
traits of a Rabbi; (2) Changes During a Rabbi's Tenure; (3) What
Makes a Leader; (4) What Motivates People; (5) The Rabbi's Role,
Influence, and Frustrations; and (6) The Rabbi and Burnout.

This is a preliminary study, but hopefully one which will
open up more avenues of serious discussion to help Rabbis and
congregants in the future.

TRAITS OF A RABBI

It is presumptuous, even dangerous, to lump all Rabbis
together and assume they are all the same. Each Rabbi is unique
and in a certain sense irreducible to stereotype. Likewise, the
Rabbi's clientele, which influences and is in turn influenced by its
Rabbi, is vastly varied. Some Rabbis cannot get their congregants
to sneeze even if they have severe colds; other Rabbis can dictate
which charity a congregant should give to and how much, and
even where and when a disciple should move. Some Rabbis lead,
others are led. Some congregants dictate, others yearn for direction. One should keep in mind the vast spectrum of difference,
personal and interactional, as one attempts to make some preliminary observations.

Studies of the psychological profile of the Rabbinate are rare.
However, one study has shown that in general, Jewish seminarians are high in the need for achievement, endurance, nurturance,
and understanding. They are low in the need for aggression,
autonomy, impulsivity, and play (Blass, 1979).

Our image of what a Rabbi should be probably would
include the following behaviour traits: extravert, enjoys people,
eager to help others, understanding and patient, tolerant of others,
of strong moral and ethical character, appreciative of his own
finiteness and fallability, among others. The general idealized
profile is of a well-integrated, secure individual.

Often, however, the profile is at odds with reality. Instead of being the outgoing personality, many Rabbis are insular, locked almost obsessively into narcissistic self-concern. They take themselves seriously, almost too seriously, to the neglect of others. This is often rationalized by the argument that no one in the Congregation really cares about the Rabbi, so the Rabbi must fend for himself. Hence, the general image of the Rabbi as a lonely figure. This perceived loneliness may stem from the fact that Rabbis often must make unpopular decisions. Yet, we cannot escape from the fact that often unpopular decisions engender or are engendered by poor Rabbi-Congregation relations.

The Congregational structure often contributes to the sense of the "separateness" of the Rabbis. The Talmud (*Nedarim*, 20b) asks, "Who are the ministering angels?" The answer given by the Talmud - "the Rabbis!" Rashi comments that Rabbis are a breed apart from ordinary people. This may corroborate the feeling of some that Rabbis are not human, even as it contradicts those who insist that Rabbis are not angels.

In the Congregational setting, the Rabbi is a breed apart. Often he is bedecked in unique garb and he preaches from on high. Anyone who does this on a continual basis cannot help but be overcome with feelings of grandeur and majesty. Like the conductor who controls the orchestra, many Rabbis feel they have the Congregation in the palm of their hand as they "preach." They often see themselves as performers on center stage who impose themselves and what they have to impart. No one dare interrupt the Rabbi, or talk in the middle of the sermon. Talking during the service is another matter, and in most shuls, not nearly as serious a breach of protocol. An almost God-like grandeur is thus "imposed" on the Rabbi.

This grandeur should not lead us to assume that the Rabbi is beyond human frailty. Aside from being lonely at the top, Rabbis also feel very vulnerable. They remain open to criticism for making controversial statements or forgetting important greetings. They feel compelled to protect their position and are alert, even over-alert, to any encroachments upon their dignity or honor. Some of the most delicate negotiations in Jewish history have concerned the touchy problems of properly slotting in another Rabbi or Rabbis with the incumbent at a Wedding, Bar Mitzvah, or testimonial.

The Rabbi, for all the prestige and power he may have, is quite often an insecure person, with a fragile ego, sensitive to any variables which may compromise his status and stature. He craves for acceptance from his Congregation. Rabbis who are well-liked by their Congregation are admired and envied by their colleagues. Rabbis thus tacitly affirm what they would overtly reject with all their vigour; namely, that it is the Congregants who render the verdict on the Rabbi's worth.

One interesting manifestation of Rabbinic insecurity is observed in how Rabbis react to comments about their performance, most frequently their speeches. Most Rabbis welcome and appreciate kudos for speeches, but are visibly upset by negative reaction. Quite often, a Rabbi who receives many compliments and one or two criticisms for his speech will more likely sulk over the negative comment and ignore or discount the positive. There are, to be sure, Rabbis who are oblivious to any critique and dismiss it as unwarranted; they accept only kind reactions.

Between the low of insecurity and high of unassailability is the middle ground of reality, a balanced position where praise is appreciated and criticism welcome. This type of balance is forthcoming only among well-integrated, secure Rabbis. Alas, the North American situation, as will be seen, is not conducive to a balanced Rabbinate, but inclines either towards the pompous or the insecure, or a combination of the two. In many respects, then, the Rabbi is just like everyone else, only more so!

CHANGES DURING RABBI'S TENURE

According to the Talmud (*Gittin*, 62a), the Rabbis are royalty. On the other hand, the Talmud asserts that the Rabbinate, or more precisely, lordship, buries its possessors (*Pesahim*, 87b). Rashi comments that this evolves because the Rabbis are haughty and do not listen to rebuke. Are Rabbis royalty, or are they unfit for their crown?

INDIVIDUAL, FAMILY, COMMUNITY:
JUDEO -PSYCHOLOGICAL PERSPECTIVES

One of the three things which shorten one's days and years
is when a person behaves in an authoritarian manner (Talmud
Berakhot, 55a). The suggestion from the commentaries, emphasizing the word "atzmo," is that this occurs either for setting up one's
self as a Rabbi rather than having the Congregation do so, or
behaving high-and-mighty even in private. These observations
reflect the need for balance in one's approach to leadership and the
requirement not to let position become person.

The Talmudic advice to hate lordship (Rabbinate) is similarly explained (Avot d'Rabbe Natan, 1:11) as meaning that a person
should not place the crown on his head by himself, rather others
should place it for him. Hasidic wisdom has it that "Love Work
and Hate Lordship" implies that if a man accepts a call to a
Rabbinic post he must consider, as the reason for his acceptance,
not the love for lordship and authority, but love of endeavor on
behalf of the community's spiritual betterment. The Rabbi is thus
forewarned to approach his tenure with trepidation, not haughti-
ness or presumptuousness. But the Rabbinate, however purely
intended, does some funny things to people.

Rabbe Yehoshua ben Prah'ya, who had been appointed
Nasi, or President of the Sanhedrin, said, "At first, whoever were
to say to me, 'take the honor,' I would have bound him and put him
in front of a lion, but now, whoever would say to me 'give up the
honor,' I would pour a kettle of boiling water on him" (Talmud,
Menahot, 109a). At first, Rabbi Yehoshua perceived the position of
authority as an onerous task in which one is constantly hounded
and badgered by the multitude. It seemed to him like being fed to
the lions! Thus would he have done to anyone who suggested he
take the position. However, if one is removed from the position,
one is an embarrassment, and there is a reddening of the face. So,
he would have poured boiling water, i.e., reddened the face, of
anyone who would have deprived him of his position.

However humble one may be in anticipation of attaining
prominence, it is quite difficult to maintain this humility throughout one's tenure. This is one of the major changes which afflicts the
idealistic Rabbi over the course of the years.

The present system for choosing Rabbis also discourages the
humble perspective from the start. Candidates vie against each

other, each trying to impress the selection committee. One cannot hold back in the face of this fierce competition. Selection committees are not interested in doubts; they are interested in total confidence and the ability to do the job.

The modern Rabbi is thus made to fit into a Madison Avenue mode, exuding confidence, talking smoothly and showing a well-rounded presence. Rabbis make a major psychological compromise even before they assume their responsibilities. They are forced to live the life others conceive for them, rather than vice-versa. There are other major negative changes which overtake the Rabbi during his tenure, most of which come under the heading of frustration with one's self and one's calling. These frustrations and how they impact on the Rabbi will be discussed later.

WHAT MAKES A LEADER

The Rabbi is, or at least is perceived to be, a leader within his community. It would be worthwhile to take a cursory look at general theories of leadership and how they relate to the Rabbi.

The "great man - great woman" theory of leadership, which attempted to hone in on leadership qualities through analysis of the traits of great leaders, has proven disappointing. No clear cut list of traits required for great leadership has been constructed. At the end of several decades of research, there seem to be almost as many different lists as there are psychologists who have worked on this issue. Thus, the tendency now is to comprehend the nature of leadership relative to situational rather than personal factors (Baron and Bryne, 1981, p. 441), be they of the leader or the group. The question of "Who becomes a leader" is best answered in terms of the task faced by the group and the general situation within which it must operate, rather than in terms of a few crucial traits possessed by specific members (Hollander & Julian, 1970).

Fred Fiedler, in his contingency model of leader effectiveness, says that two of the most important factors in a leader's success in directing his or her group are: (1) the leader's personal traits or characteristics and (2) certain features of the situation. Some leaders are primarily concerned with task performance. They tend to behave in a directing, authoritarian manner. Others seem to be more concerned with establishing warm, friendly relations with other members and behave in a less directing, relaxed and friendly fashion. According to Fiedler, both of these two approaches are good, depending on the situation. The directing, authoritarian approach may be effective under conditions that are either very favourable or very unfavourable to the leader. In contrast, a non-directing, friendly leadership style may be more successful under conditions that are moderately favourable or unfavourable.

The reasoning behind this is as follows. When conditions are moderately favourable, a friendly, non-directive style can help smooth over differences of opinion and improve cooperation. Thus, a non-directing leadership style would be best. However, when conditions are highly unfavourable a directing, authoritarian style is needed. Without it the group may fall apart. And when conditions are extremely favourable, an authoritarian style may also prove effective, since group members are confident of attaining their goals and would be willing to accept orders from an authoritative leader. What conditions determine the extent to which a given situation is relatively favourable or unfavourable to the leader? Fiedler suggests three factors;
1. The leader's personal relationships with other group members;
2. The extent to which group tasks are clearly structured;
3. The power of the leader over other group members (Fiedler & Chemers, 1974).

It must be left to the individual Rabbi to decide which condition best describes his congregation and his own relation to it. It would seem that most Rabbis, upon assuming a post, are in a testing-the-waters phase, which best corresponds to a "moderately favourable" condition. Such a condition argues in favour of a friendly, non-directive style.

Rabbis who build congregations from scratch will likely be surrounded by those who appreciate them, moderate disciples of sorts. With this solid backing, authoritative Rabbinating may be possible. Authoritative Rabbinating is certainly the rule among Hasidic groups where the Rabbi usually is in a "highly favourable" position.

While Fiedler correlates highly unfavourable conditions with the directing, authoritarian style - a combination one sees not infrequently in the Rabbinate - it is unclear which comes first, the unfavourable conditions or the authoritaraian style. Whatever the case, once this style has taken hold, the Rabbi and Congregation are in an unfortunate position where change is probably the best alternative for all concerned.

There is more to Rabbinic leadership than the Fiedler model. The Talmud makes two apparently contradictory comments concerning leadership. In one, it says that the Divine presence rests only on a person who is wise, strong, rich and of stature (*Nedarim*, 38a); in another, it states that God does not shine Divine presence or rest Divine presence except on a person who is wise, strong, rich, and modest (*Shabbat*, 92a). Why in the one instance is the fourth category a person of stature and in the other, the fourth category is modesty? These are apparent opposites.

Perhaps the key is that in the one statement we speak about the Divine presence resting and, in the other, God placing it on. God places it on an individual who is modest and who does not seek greatness. However, once having been blessed, the individual, however modest, becomes a person of stature who is respected within the community. There is a need to balance off the modesty an individual has with responsibility to community. That is to say, modesty does not mean thinking of the self as nothing; rather one thinks of one's self in a balanced perspective, as an individual who can serve but is not compelled to thrust ego needs to the fore. A person of stature is a person who is at peace with the self and aware that what is being done for the community is service rather than glory.

In this regard, *wisdom* or to know how to behave, *strength*, or not to compromise principle, and *wealth*, or not to be beholden or intimidated by those who pay for the wages, are all essential.

Rabbinic leadership is also friendship on a mass scale. One must be sensitive to the collective and individual needs of the congregation and respond to them in the appropriate manner. The Rabbinic counseling of today is essentially a modern label attached to the age-old Rabbinic savvy for giving the right advice at the right time.

INDIVIDUAL, FAMILY, COMMUNITY:
JUDEO -PSYCHOLOGICAL PERSPECTIVES

Leadership is seen as a two-way street. Many studies suggest that leaders' behaviour is often strongly affected by the actions and demands of other group members (Beckhouse, et. al., 1975; Fodor, 1978). This has become known as the transactional view. In this view, leadership is seen as a reciprocal process of social influence in which leaders both direct followers and are, in turn, influenced by them. This also calls attention to the importance of the perceptions of both leaders and followers regarding the relationship between them.

The Talmud says that the generation follows according to the leader, or that the leader follows according to the generation (*Arakhin*, 17a). The difference of opinion seems to revolve around· matters of temperament which are affected reflexively by either the generation or the leader.

The Rabbi-Congregation dialectic of the modern era has its host of particular nuances which influence the nature of the Rabbinate. Not only temperament but many other facets of Rabbinic life are intertwined in the North American Synagogue system.

A Hasid asked Rabbi Bunam: There is a Talmudic allegory that God showed to Adam each generation and its leaders. Why did God first show the generation and then the leaders? Rabbi Bunam replied: Had God shown him the leaders first, Adam would have exclaimed, "Should a man such as Bunam be a leader?" But Adam saw the generation first, and then said; "In such a generation Bunam is worthy to be a leader."

In a peculiar way, the Congregations of today are getting the Rabbis they deserve, and vice-versa. Transaction at its best - or worst - depending on the situation.

Leadership capacities increase with maturity. It would thus seem appropriate for Congregations to prefer older Rabbis and for Rabbis to defer entering the Rabbinate until having become "sage with age." But this is not the case, and the fruits of Rabbinic labour in the contemporary setting are often hazardous. Thus, the Ropshitzer heard that Rabbi Zvi Elimelekh of Dinov had become a Rabbi. In great displeasure, the Rabbi remarked that the Dinover had acted foolishly. When he was pressed for an explanation, the

Ropshitzer said; "Every leader is allotted by heaven a term of service lasting for a certain number of years. Had the Dinover waited to commence his term at a more mature age, he would have enjoyed a longer life." It happened exactly as the Rabbi had surmised. The Dinover was summoned by death while still young.

Today's Rabbi, in need of an income, cannot wait for "later." Many Congregations would not even consider anyone over forty as a serious candidate. It is generally known that the life expectancy of a Congregational Rabbi is less than the average. Aside from quantitative concerns, there are qualitative concerns, or problems which plague the Rabbi in the struggle to satisfy his calling and his membership. Many Rabbis may be too young to do an adequate job and, once having matured through on-the-job, albeit unhappy training, may be too old for the positions merited by their talents. It is a frustrating conundrum which must be appreciated if we are to achieve any improvement in the North American Rabbinate.

There is, however, one saving grace of an ultimate nature. The Talmud says that "Anyone who benefits the multitudes, no sin will come through that person. What is the reason for this? In order that he should not be in hell whilst his disciples are in paradise" (Yoma, 87a).

On balance, our concerns here should be placed into proper perspective. The Rabbi's present may be tenuous, but his future seems more secure.

WHAT MOTIVATES PEOPLE

Any study of leadership must focus on what techniques or approaches will induce people to change, preferably for the better.

One important element in this regard is the need to be aware of the clientele. A good glimpse at the state of North American society came in a survey conducted by Psychology Today, reported in the issue of November 1981. This obviously involves readers who are of a higher intelligence than the normal population. Ninety-three percent admitted driving faster than the speed limit;

eighty-eight percent told little white lies in the past year; sixty-eight percent had taken home office supplies or other materials; sixty-seven percent cheated on examinations or assignments; sixty percent parked illegally; forty-seven percent took sick days from work even though well enough to go to work; forty-five percent had extra-marital affairs; forty-one percent drove while drunk or under the influence of drugs; thirty-eight percent tried to save money on tax returns by lying or withholding information; thirty-eight percent had gone through customs purposely not declaring an item; thirty-seven percent made long distance telephone calls at work; thirty-three percent deceived a best friend about something important in the past year; twenty-eight percent cheated on an expense account in the past year; and nineteen percent cut into line or failed to wait for a turn in a public place (Hassett, 1981).

One may say that at least these people are very honest about their cheating! However, this points to some important ethical dilemmas in our society which have also invaded the Jewish population. They pose a serious problem for any leader trying to project a sense of honesty and sincerity in approaching life's responsibilities. In the *Psychology Today* survey the very religious scored best on all issues - they lied less, withheld less taxes, deceived less, and parked less illegally. However, the real problem lies in self-reporting. Very often, religious individuals justify their own behaviour, or even hide it, in order to come forth as clean. We do not really understand the relationship between religion and moral behaviour.

Other studies have shown that religious individuals do not score so well on Kohlberg's moral development scale (Stevens, Blank & Poushinsky, 1977). Many people may be caught in a behavioural syndrome of "follow the leader," or follow the follower. When we see other persons engage in prohibited actions that we too would like to perform, our restraint or inhibitions against doing so may be sharply reduced (Rosenthal & Zimmerman, 1978). A study by economist Michael W. Spicer and psychologist Sven B. Lundstedt (Maital, 1982) revealed that "the more tax evaders the tax payer knows, the more likely he is to evade taxes himself." Tax evasion or cheating on tax returns is contagious. It was, perhaps, in recognition of this general societal malaise that Viktor Frankl remarked: *"Humane* humans are, and probably will always remain, a minority. But it is precisely for this reason that each of us is challenged to *join* the minority. Things are bad. But unless we do our best to improve them, everything will become worse" (Frankl, 1975, p. 84).

To improve things, to motivate people to change, is not easy. When challenged, we tend to justify past behaviour and reaffirm it rather than acknowledge deficiency and express willingness to change. Insecurity breeds protectionism, in which people remain entrenched in their positions, unwilling to transcend themselves. What can be done to shake people loose?

One factor in bringing out the intrinsic good of people is mood. The general feeling is that when individuals are in a good mood they are much more likely to be altruistic (Cunningham, Steinberg & Grev, 1980). An experiment was conducted by Isen and Levin (1972) in which positive feelings were created by experimenters placing a dime in the coin return slots for the next telephone user to find, and then comparing the altruistic behaviour of those who had just found money and those who had not. Just near the phone booth a female confederate waited until the subject completed the call, and managed to drop a folder full of papers directly in the subject's path. Amazingly, less than five percent of the shoppers who had simply made the phone calls stopped to help the stranger. But when they had just found a dime, the percentage jumped to ninety percent who stopped and helped.

Congregations which regularly offer sumptuous kiddushim may have inadvertently stumbled onto an effective strategy!

On the other side, the element of fear can be a decisive motivator. Results of many studies suggest that under certain conditions, strong fear can facilitate change of attitude. As an example, a frightening film of diseased lungs and actual lung operations has produced greater shifts in smokers' attitudes to their habit than milder films showing smoking machines or charts and graphs (Leventhal, Watts, & Pagano, 1967). In particular, it appears that appeals based on fear need the following conditions to effect change in attitude:

1. The appeal should be quite strong;
2. The persons who receive the appeal believe the dangers shown are likely to occur;
3. Those persons believe that the recommendations for avoiding the dangers presented in the message will prove effective. (Mewborn & Rogers, 1979).

Appeals to the Jewish community, be it for Israel or for institutions, usually invoke the element of fear, fear for the survival of Israel or fear that an institution will be forced to close, if monetary assistance is not forthcoming.

In *Numbers* (1:20-47), the population of the tribes is enumerated. Tribal size ranged anywhere from thirty-two thousand to seventy-four thousand males above the age of twenty. The tribe of Levi, from the age of thirty and up, numbered only about eight and a half thousand (*Numbers*, 4:48). Their count from one month and up was only twenty-two thousand (*Numbers*, 3:39). Thus, the Levitic tribe did not proliferate at the rate of the rest of Israel, contrary to what one would have expected from the holiest of tribes.

Nahmanides, commenting on this, indicates that the Levites, as is well known, did not fall for Pharaoh's trap and were not included in the servitude. As far as the rest of Israel is concerned, we are told that the more they were afflicted the more they multiplied (*Exodus*, 1:12). God wanted to show the Egyptians that the Almighty was more powerful and no matter what Egypt did to control the numbers of the people of Israel, they could not succeed; all their efforts were counterproductive. However, since the Levites were not included in the edict of Pharaoh, no extraordinary multiplication measures were implemented for them (Nahmanides, *Numbers*, 3:14).

There is also another possibility, as suggested through Nahmanides, namely a psychological dimension to this theological interpretation. The Israelites, in general, refuse to buckle under to threats and scare tactics. When their existence is in jeopardy, they respond with alacrity and dispatch. The Levites were never threatened, so they went about their business as usual. The others, as they were separated husband from wife, resorted to all means of conjugal closeness in order to have more children. Thus, they multiplied more than they would have under normal circumstances. This affords us an insight into what makes a community work. A community works on the basis of a reaction to emergency or to crisis.

Population attrition is, in fact, one of the major crises facing Judaism today. And, even though all three elements in effecting change suggested by Mewborn and Rogers are present, in that (1) the appeal is strong, (2) people believe the dangers are likely to occur, and (3) the recommendations are perceived to be effective, little is actually changing.

Rabbis preach that there is less than zero growth among the Jewish population, that the dangers are real and ominous, and that a higher birth rate is the only real solution. Yet things are not improving. One reason may be that families today "plan" how many children they will have and the plans are based on priorities, including economic circumstance, career preference, and narcissistic concerns. Entrenched plans change only with great difficulty. Another is that each individual thinks only in personal terms and that his or her "one more" is insignificant. This points to one of the fundamental weaknesses in messages directed to the mass - each member of the mass thinks that only the others are meant. The result is that little changes.

Following the covenantal experience reported in Nitzavim, Moshe Rabbenu, according to the Abravanel, went (Vayelekh Moshe) (*Deuteronomy*, 31:1) to every tribe with the message of the covenant. It seems peculiar that in the very last days of his life Moshe would have expended his energies on a matter that had already been taken care of and which now seemed repetitive. Since the entire community had heard Moshe's covenantal message, what it demanded of them, as well as what was promised for them, why was it now necessary to go to every tribe?

The fact that Moshe went to this trouble in one of the final gestures of his life indicates that he considered it quite vital. He recognized a weakness which usually obtains in addressing a mass. Everyone hears, everyone listens, but not everyone interprets correctly. When a mass is exhorted to action, most people in the mass think the exhortation is addressed to everyone else, but not to them. Moshe was singularly aware of this natural propensity of the masses. He feared that the impact of the covenant would be lost. He therefore went to the trouble of delivering the covenant's message to each super family or tribe, telling them that in their specialties, whether it be in study, business, or charity, they were unique, but nevertheless part of an overall framework in which no individual or family of individuals could evade their responsibility.

Whether it is through creating a good mood or convincing the community that a crisis exists, Rabbinic leadership will succeed only to the extent it impresses upon the individuals who make up the community that *they* are being addressed, *they* are being challenged, and *they* must respond.

THE RABBI'S ROLE, INFLUENCE AND FRUSTRATIONS

According to one observer, the role of the Rabbi "is primarily to help the individual Jew and Jewish community relate 'Jewishly' to the awe and mystery of life, and to live comfortably as Jews amidst our non-Jewish fellow citizens. That role requires that we be first and foremost students and thinkers - students, not professional scholars; thinkers, not academic philosophers" (S. Greenberg, 1975, p. 122).

One may quarrel with this definition of the Rabbi's role. However, the general thrust is almost a motherhood statement, that Rabbis are primarily obliged to bring their congregations to the central core of Jewish life in all its dimensions. The duty of Rabbinic leadership is to bring people to levels of understanding, commitment, and action they could not attain on their own.

It is useful for Rabbis to see themselves as students, always willing to learn, just as it is useful to see one's self as less than perfect, and thus receptive to constructive criticism. In the words of Rabbi Nahman of Bratzlav - "He who cannot accept reproof cannot become a great man." Rabbis cannot be ivory tower recluses, "but leaders with whom the people can identify, whose knowledge and spiritual and ethical integrity they respect, and in whose personal lives and spoken and written word they find helpful guidance for their own lives as human beings and as Jews" (ibid., p. 123). The Rabbi should be a friend one can feel free to call upon in need.

Unfortunately, idealistic theory is often far removed from reality. "There are already many Rabbis in the field who by temperament or adaptation have frozen into the administrator-fund raiser-benediction giver-pattern. After years of non-use, talents for reading and studying may atrophy" (I. Greenberg, 1975, p. 127). Quite possibly, the Rabbi of today is burdened with too much extra-Rabbinical work which must be done, and thus has little time to do that which should be done.

It has been observed that one rarely hears of new large Orthodox Shuls being established in major cities, as the constituency for such synagogues has diminished appreciably (Kelman, 1975, p. 81). In the light of one observer's recommendation that the ratio of families per Rabbi must be lowered if the Rabbi's job is to be done right (I. Greenberg, 1975, p. 128), this should be welcome news. There is, however, an economic catch-22 here. Small congregations pay lower salaries, thus forcing their Rabbis to seek outside jobs (usually teaching) to raise their incomes. In working outside the congregation, however, one's time and energy for congregational endeavour are reduced. The frustration and sense of inadequacy which result from Rabbis feeling they are not doing an adequate job has become an occupational hazard.

The individual Rabbi feels a sense of dissatisfaction and impotence in communal affairs for a few reasons. First, there is a lack of faith in the supreme importance of the synagogue and the Rabbi within the total communal structure. Second, there is a profoundly felt sense of failure to adequately meet the people's needs for an intelligible and acceptable philosophy of life as Jews. This has evolved because professional duties have become so numerous that Rabbis do not have the time and energy to devote themselves to this task (S. Greenberg, 1975, p. 120-121).

The Rabbi's difficulty in attaining acceptability as leader for communal policy may betray the feeling that the Rabbi represents a special interest group, the constituency of God, and does not reflect the feelings of the broad-based community. The Rabbi is tolerated and often humoured, but is not respected as Rabbi. Those Rabbis who have a measure of influence in communal affairs have gained this clout by virtue of their own personal efforts, and are respected more in spite of the fact they are Rabbis rather than because they are Rabbis.

The Rabbi, within his congregation, has a captive audience. It is folly, however, for any Rabbi to overemphasize the importance of speeches. They may impress people who will come back for more entertainment, but it is doubtful whether a Rabbi actually shapes a congregation or influences them toward change. Some Rabbis have the charisma, energy and commitment to exert such influence, but they are the exceptional ones.

The Rabbi is often the model through which individuals vicariously live out and through their religion. This may come as a surprise to some Rabbis, but one need only recall the special relationships which develop between not-so-religious individuals and their Rabbis. These individuals do not change their ways, but they remain close, even staunch supporters of the Rabbi. It is as if the Rabbi lives religion for them, and they, who latch on to the Rabbi, achieve salvation by association. Vicarious religion, admittedly, is not a Jewish concept, and is another instance of a non-Jewish concept foisting itself upon the Jewish community. Nevertheless, it is a reality.

According to Rabbe Shmuel bar Nahmayni, whatever the leaders of the generation do, the generation itself, its constituency, also does. How so? If the president, Nasi, permits, the head of the court says - "if the leader has permitted, how can I forbid it?" The rest of the children of their generation say - "the judges have permitted, how can we forbid it?" Who has caused the entire generation to sin? The leader who initiated it in the first place (*Midrash Rabbah*, Deuteronomy, 2:12).

Notice that the example concerns permitting that which is forbidden. This is another sphere of Rabbinic influence, *where*, prohibition is ignored but permission eagerly followed. The frustrated *apikores* of the Talmud brands the Rabbis as impotent, never permitting the raven or forbidding the dove (*Sanhedrin*, 99b). The complaint may seem balanced, but in reality Rabbinic prohibitions tend to be theoretical rather than practical matters. Since people do as they feel anyway, permissions are escalated into norms. Whatever pangs of conscience one may have about an issue are immediately relieved by Rabbinic license. It is as if the person now feels no hesitancy about explaining the action to God. "Why blame me, my Rabbi gave me permission!" The Rabbi, like the Nasi in Rabbe Shmuel bar Nahmayni's construct, is a spiritual dumping ground.

On an individual level, people hide behind Rabbinic allowance. On a communal level, people seek out the Rabbi who most represents their own preconceived notions or interests. In previous generations, the miracle making Zaddikim, including those who lived in great luxury, appealed to the poor, unsophisticated, lower middle class of the small towns, whereas the scholarly Zaddikim who spurned magical practices appealed to the wealthier and more educated strata. Most Jews were able to find the Hasidic group congruent with their economic position, social status, educational level and style of life (Sharot, 1980, p. 335).

The ambivalent American Jew, in the modern context, chooses that part of the tradition which is compatible with his/her own special interests and raises those interests to the level of ideology, pressing them upon society in universalistic terms. Those of the far right do the same with specific stringencies. Both groups will use, even abuse the Rabbi, to reinforce an entrenched position. The penchant for self justification works wonders for the insecure North American Jew.

The Talmud, recognizing the precarious position of the Rabbi, asserts that in the same way as it is an obligation to say that which will be obeyed, so, too, is it an obligation to desist from saying that which will not be heeded (*Yevamot*, 65b). Another view is that it is an obligation (to desist), not merely a mitzvah; mitzvah in this sense is used by the Talmud to indicate not commandment but good advice. The reasoning is that if you rebuke a scoffer he will probably hate you, thus causing him to transgress the prohibition against hating. One commentary (Etz Yosef) insists that this only applies to that which is not explicit in the Torah, such as adding extra minutes on to Yom Kippur (*Ein Yaakov*, 1955, p. 28).

In another statement relative to this issue, the Talmud observes that if a scholar is loved by the town's people, their love is not due to his superiority but to the fact that he does not rebuke them for neglecting spiritual matters (*Ketuvot*, 105b). This relates to the idea that we should not rebuke scoffers because they may hate us. The commentaries take the view that most people in a city (congregational setting?) are not wise men who may love and appreciate rebuke; rather they lean more towards the other side, being scoffers or individuals who are not serious about their responsibilities in life.

Rabbis are thus given some leeway and are not under an unbending obligation to browbeat. Where change is unlikely to result, popularity or being liked is seen as a positive value because it forges a closeness between Rabbi and Congregation which may bode well for the future.

In the contemporary setting, most Congregations react negatively to *musar*, to being told off. They do not want to be burdened with "guilt trips."

In general, Congregations do not appreciate Rabbis who make them feel uncomfortable about themselves. They want their selves to be reaffirmed rather than denied. Rabbinic influence and hence, frustration, is forced to work within this major constraint.

The Rabbi's job is a transient one. It is not unusual for a traditional Rabbi to have passed through six positions by the time he is sixty years old (Carlin & Mendlovitz, 1976, p. 173). Rabbis try to impress in order to gain some measure of job stability, but often, they try too hard to impress. Impressionism becomes a part of the daily lexicon. The irony is that in the desire, and sometimes desperation, to plant roots, the Rabbi's home life becomes chaotic and his immediate family winds up hating the Rabbinate as well as the congregants who are seen as the trouble makers.

The Rabbi with problems in the congregation usually suffers because of a few rabble rousers, as opposed to facing a broad-based malaise. Sometimes the vocal few can create the general malaise. The two major problem types within the Congregation are: (1) the know-it-alls, who think they know more than the Rabbi. Ex-Yeshiva students, or those who have just returned to the fold, are often a Rabbi's nightmare instead of a blessing; (2) the congregant with ego problems who, frustrated at work and at home, seeks to carve his niche in the shul, sometimes by carving the Rabbi to bits.

Because they pay the Rabbi's salary, some congregants feel they own him, and the Rabbi must be their puppet. Establishing a balance within the Rabbi's community is a most delicate task, demanding insight, patience, and tolerance.

The Rabbi who becomes overwhelmed by unanticipated problems confronting him, problems which prevent him from fulfilling his Rabbinic calling, becomes a candidate for a condition commonly referred to as burnout.

THE RABBI AND BURNOUT

What is burnout? Burnout is a state of mind that can afflict those who work with other people. This happens often, but not exclusively, in the helping professions, among those who receive much less from their clients, supervisors, and colleagues than they give. It is "the result of constant or repeated *emotional pressure* associated with an intense involvement with people over long periods of time" (Pines, Aronson & Kafry, 1981, p. 15).

The behavioural cluster associated with burnout includes exhaustion, detachment, boredom and cynicism, impatience and irritability, suspicion of being unappreciated, paranoia, disorientation, psychosomatic complaints, and depression (Freudenberger & Richelson, 1981, pp. 62-68).

"The people who start out with the highest ideals...are likely to experience the most severe burnout" (Pines, Aronson & Kafry, 1981, p. 34). The irony of burnout is that precisely those individuals who are idealistic and meaning-oriented are most susceptible to burnout. Bluntly put, "In order to burnout a person needs to have been on fire at one time" (ibid.).

Professionals who devote many years to study and training for a career enter with the expectation that the career will provide a steady challenge and opportunity for self-actualization. However, when their talents and skills are stifled, when their expectations do not materialize, they become candidates for burnout (Pines, Aronson & Kafry, p. 154). Additionally, in such areas as social services - and the Rabbinate, in a broad sense, fits into this category - the flow of emotions is usually one-sided, from worker to client. This further exacerbates emotional depletion, with any emotional "refill" highly unlikely.

Rabbis, too, are idealistic and approach their obligations with eagerness, responsibleness, and the desire to fulfill and be fulfilled. However, Rabbis and other professionals often suffer from the failure to have their efforts recognized and acknowledged.

According to Pines, Aronson & Kafry (1981, p. 55), the most idealistic and highly committed social servants are the ones who have the greatest difficulty detaching themselves and, as a result, tend to burnout relatively soon (p. 55). Burnout, specifically Rabbinical burnout, is the end result of the host of problems and frustrations previously enumerated. It is the depressed state resulting from unrealized expectations, frustrated hopes, neutralized idealism, and the inability, born of a deep commitment, to detach oneself from the situation.

There is an auxiliary aspect of burnout, what I refer to as "Burnout fallout." The first and most vulnerable area for burnout fallout is the home. The "I don't care" attitude linked to burnout invades the home and affects the children, who cannot comprehend their father's harshness, irritability and emotional distancing. The wife is probably most affected, as she feels the pain the most and is hardly able to lift her husband out of his rut, probably because she is in the rut with him. The following describes how many Rabbis' wives may feel about their position.

> The Rabbi's wife should be attractive, but not too much so; have nice clothes, but not too nice (she will always be applauded for making her clothes); have a nice basic hair-do, but not too nice; be friendly, but not too friendly; be aggressive and greet everyone, especially visitors, but not too aggressive; intelligent, but not too intelligent; educated, but not too educated; down-to-earth, but not too much so; capable, but not too capable; charming, but not too charming; and be herself — but not openly. (Faulkner, 1981, p. 24)

The Rabbi thus cannot rely on his wife to help him out of the burnout condition, and is doubly frustrated because he often cannot share his depression with others. The Rabbi is there to help others deal with their depression but he himself is not allowed to become depressed. This pressure-cooker situation only makes a bad circumstance worse. Burnout affects not only Rabbis who are frustrated, but also eminently successful Rabbis who cannot handle the constant pressure.

Although the term burnout is relatively new, there is reason to believe that burnout has been with us for many generations. Here it is useful to explore why Moshe Rabbenu did not merit leading Israel into the promised land.

There were two episodes in which Moshe was asked to draw water from a rock. In the Refidim episode (*Exodus*, 17:1-7), he was asked to smite the rock to bring forth water for the people to drink. In the Kadesh episode (*Numbers*, 20:2-13), he was asked to bring forth water to the people from the rock and *give* them and their cattle to drink. In the Refidim instance Moshe was not asked to become personally involved. He was asked to smite the rock, let the water come out and then let the people drink. In the Kadesh episode he was asked to be involved personally, to give the congregation and the cattle to drink. Why the difference? Because the Refidim episode was a rebellion and the reaction was to be a commensurately detached approach, but the Kadesh episode was not necessarily a rebellion, rather an expression of the people's desire to survive in order to be God's nation.

Is it out of bounds to propose that God saw the Kadesh situation as an opportunity to develop a closeness, to project a filial love for the people, to give them a manifestation of concern which would inspire them, even take them out of their depression and frustration, and at the same time prepare them with a spiritual uplifting for impending entry into the promised land? This could have been projected with a pronounced impact had Moshe talked to the rock, brought forth the water, and personally seen to it that the people drank. Such paternalistic care would have been interpreted as God's care transmitted through Moshe. It would have sanctified God within the congregation.

Instead, however, Moshe and Aaron approached the people angrily. Rather than talking to the rock, Moshe struck the rock, not once but twice, projecting the apparent anger of God and then, in perhaps the most important statement, water came forth abundantly and the congregation drank and their cattle. Moshe did not offer them the water to drink; he acted with as much detachment here as in Refidim and, perhaps, understandably so.

The years Moshe spent with the Israelites in Egypt and in the wilderness were not easy years. He had persevered through complaints against God, challenges to his authority and repeated attacks on the foundations of the Israelite community. His reaction in Kadesh could, perhaps, be seen as the straw that broke the camel's back, or at the very least, in the background of the constant confrontations he had with the people. Had it been the first time, he would have been patient. But this was not the first rebellious occasion. It was quite obvious from the way Moshe handled the situation that his patience with the people had dried up.

Therefore, God said to him and Aaron that because they had not believed in God, to sanctify God in the eyes of the children of Israel, they would not bring this assembly into the land which had been given to them. There is no indication of a sin on the part of Moshe and Aaron, but rather a diminished confidence or trust in the people. God had projected to them an understanding of the people's complaint, that this situation should be handled with delicate care, and would thus be best mediated. The fact is that Moshe's patience had run so dry so that he could not accept God's appreciation of the situation. This was not a rebellion against God or a rejection of God, but rather an indication that Moshe could no longer tolerate the people's challenges.

God was sanctified through the situation, nonetheless, in that the people were miraculously delivered from their plight. But this sanctification came in spite of the action of Moshe and Aaron, not because of their action. God recognized that the generation entering the promised land was a new generation whose behaviour could not be judged in the light of their ancestors. Such a generation would need a new leader who would be tolerant and patient. Therefore, he told Moshe that he was not the one to bring them to this new situation. A new leader, unencumbered by previous deviances, could cope more capably with the people. At the risk of being reductionistic, it seems clear that what happened at Kadesh indicated that Moshe had burnt out as a leader.

It must be emphasized that the situation of Moshe Rabbenu is not exactly comparable with the contemporary Rabbinate and that his burnout was of a different sort. The apparently high incidence of burnout among Rabbis today is related to many factors, some of which cannot be compared to the situation of Moshe Rabbenu.

The host of problems discussed previously can be put under the broad heading of "A Rabbinical career which does not live up to expectations." This, however, does not fully get to the root of the matter. Granted that most Rabbis enter the field saturated with idealism, many still see the Rabbinate as a career, not merely a calling. It is a profession and, not surprisingly, has gone the way of other professions, into the burnout trap.

The difference between career and calling is, at once, the difference between self-fulfillment and self-transcendence. A Rabbinate that is embarked upon to fulfill needs and in which the transcendent perspective is of diminished importance is a burnout-producing Rabbinate. The self-defeating nature of this approach, be it to one's job or to life iteslf, was pointed out long before burnout became an issue by Viktor Frankl, who asserted that;

> The real aim of human existence cannot be found in what is called self-actualization. Human existence is essentially self-transcendence rather than self-actualization. Self-actualization is not a possible aim at all, for the simple reason that the more a man would strive for it, the more he would miss it. For only to the extent to which man commits himself to the fulfillment of his life's meaning, to this extent he also actualizes himself. In other words, self-actualization cannot be attained if it is made an end itself, but only as a side effect of self-transcendence. (Frankl, 1963, p. 175)

Education for the Rabbinate should be education toward self-transcendence and the Transcendent, because of spiritual and psychological necessity.

The Rabbinical burnout candidate often feels entrapped, lonely, and melancholy. Rabbis should take note of the fact that while individuals in organizations hunger for appreciation and often feel unappreciated, they almost never reach out to show appreciation of someone else's work. It has been found that one of the best ways for individuals to encourage others to pay attention to their work is to start acknowledging the good work of others. When individuals, on their own, reach out to give each other needed support and needed appreciation, the reaching out mushrooms and grows exponentially (Pines, Aronson & Kafry, 1981, p. 12).

The Rabbi, who is presumed to be expert at reaching out, would be well-advised to follow this suggestion. Complimenting congregational members may not always be reciprocated, but it will engender a more positive atmosphere and deflect from the tendency to be obsessed with one's own plight.

For the Rabbinical burnout problem to be solved reasonably, it must be recognized as a two-way street, in which the congregation reveres its leaders and the leaders are patient with their congregation (Talmud, *Sanhedrin*, 8a). At the same time, the Rabbis must take the lead. We should contemplate setting up a no-nonsense task force to investigate the structure of the modern Rabbinate and map out guidelines of newly defined Rabbinical responsibilities which bring out the best in North American synagogues. Ultimately, however, it remains for each Rabbi to solve his particular problem, burnout or otherwise.

The Talmud insists that even in a time of danger a person should not change from his Rabbinic majestic bearing (*Sanhedrin*, 92b). Rashi explains that Hananya, Mishael and Azarya wore their majestic clothing when forced to walk through the furnace, not to appear frightened of their enemy. Maharsha avers that the Talmudic statement means that people should not moan over their fate; they should accept it in joy and in dignity.

Applied to the modern Rabbi, who must often walk not through the furnace, but through potential burnout, it is a call to rise above the fray, not to moan but to grow, not to wear the cloak of self-fulfillment, but rather to wear the majestic Rabbinic cloak of self-transcendence. By accepting in dignity, even joy, the Rabbi ironically, even instantaneously, enhances his condition.

CHAPTER 11

THE PSYCHOLOGY OF CONVERSION

The question of the fundamental Judaic attitude to conversion is, by its very nature, controversial. It divides into two schools of thought and into differing time periods of Jewish history. Historically, there have been times when Jews indulged in missionary activity, such as in the period immediately following the destruction of the second Temple. At other times, such as during the reign of David and Solomon, conversion was severely discouraged. The reason for the negative view of conversion during the time of David and Solomon was based on the fear that conversion was merely a matter of convenience (Talmud, *Yevamot*, 24b). At that time, Judaism flowered and flourished and it was seen to be advantageous to be Jewish.

The two sides of the conversion controversy are not merely historical poles, but also philosophical opposites. The thesis and antithesis are best manifested in the interpretation of the famous Talmudic statement that "Proselytes are as hard for Israel as a sore" (*Yevamot*, 47b). The simple meaning of the phrase and the one adopted and espoused by the anti-conversion schools argues that converts are outsiders who, with exception, cannot be loyal Jews. They are thus only sores, festering blotches intruding on the

Jewish family. This observation of the Talmud may be a statement of fact rather than a causal truth. The Talmud may have been reacting to the quisling-like invasion of Jewish ranks rather than condemning all converts in advance. After all, some of Judaism's greatest heros, including Abraham, Ruth, Rabbe Akiva, Onkeles, Avtalyon, and Rabbe Meir either were, or emanated from, proselytes. In fact, strictly speaking, every single Jew stems from proselytes, since the experience of revelation on Mount Sinai was itself a mass conversion experience!

There is another interpretation of the Talmudic reference to proselytes as sores given by a well-known convert of the 12th century, R. Avraham. He contends that what the Talmud suggests is that proselytes, because they are more observant than the majority of those born as Jews, become an irritating sore and expose the guilty consciences of Jews. A seemingly disparaging comment is thus transmuted into a compliment.

ATTITUDE TO CONVERSION

Generally, the tenor of the Talmud concerning conversion is positive. Thus, the Talmud asserts that God "did not exile Israel among the nations save in order that proselytes might join them" (*Pesahim*, 87b). This does not necessarily imply the desirability of missionary activity, although those who are inclined to missionize would undoubtedly use or abuse this statement. What the Talmud suggests is that had Israel been localized in its own restricted environment, the essence of Judaism would not have travelled the world and people would not have even been aware of the beauty of Judaism. The fact of exile spreads the Judaic base over a more global spread, and thus at least gives others the opportunity to contemplate Judaism, but certainly not to be forced into it.

According to Maimonides (*Mishnah Torah, Laws of Tendencies*, 6:4), the Biblical obligation to love the proselyte is written in the same language as the obligation to love God, Who is described in the Bible as loving proselytes. God's love of converts undoubtedly stems from the obvious fact that the convert's adoption of Judaism is an exercise of choice, a choice based on perceiving the profundity and meaning of Judaism, whereas the Jew who affirms Judaism is often merely a captive of parental heritage. This association should, once and for all, clearly establish the affirmative stance of Judaism to converts.

Despite this, the anti-convert school is still quite vociferous, and tends to dominate the attitudes of Jews, even though it involves an odd conglomerate of pseudotheology and ethnic protectionism.

What is involved in conversion to Judaism? The best way to describe the process is to quote the Talmud:

If at the present time a man desires to become a proselyte, he is to be addressed as follows: What reason have you for desiring to become a proselyte; do you not know that Israel at the present time is persecuted and oppressed, despised, harassed and overcome by afflictions? If he replies, "I know and yet am unworthy," he is accepted forthwith, and is given instruction in some of the minor and some of the major commandments. He is informed of the sin involving neglect of the commandments of Gleanings, the Forgotten Sheaf, the Corner, and the Poor Man's Tithe. He is also told of the punishment for the transgression of the commandments. Furthermore, he is addressed thusly: "Be it known to you that before you came to this condition, if you had eaten suet you would not have been punishable with premature death (Karet); if you had profaned the Sabbath you would not have been punishable with stoning; but now were you to eat suet you would be punished with premature death (Karet); were you to profane the Sabbath you would be punished with stoning." And as he is informed of the punishment for the transgression of the commandments, so is he informed of the reward granted for their fulfillment... And they do not increase upon him nor enter with him into details (to discourage him too much). If he accepts, he is circumcized immediately... As soon as he is healed arrangements are made for his immediate ritual immersion, when two learned men must stand by his side and acquaint him with some of the minor commandments and some of the major ones. When he comes up after his immersion he is considered an Israelite in all respects. In the case of a woman proselyte, women have her sit in the water up to her neck, while two learned men stand outside and give her instruction in some

171

REUVEN P. BULKA

of the minor commandments and some of the major ones. (*Yevamot*, 47a-47b)

The Talmud further analyzes this simple recitation of procedure. The prospective convert is notified of minor and major commandments in order to make him aware of what he is embracing, so that he should not become a Jew under false pretenses. If he is to withdraw, he should do so beforehand.

The specific mention of commandments regarding gleaning, the forgotten sheaf, the corner, and the poor man's tithe, all relate to monetary obligations for every Jew. The prospective convert will now have to share of his material goods. Since most people protect their possessions, this is considered a good acid test of whether the candidate for conversion is really serious. However, once the sincerity of the convert is established, the convert is not to be dissuaded excessively. Rather, the convert is circumcized forthwith because, in the words of the Talmud, "The performance of a commandment must in no way be delayed" (*Yevamot*, 47b).

After ritual immersion, the candidate is a full-fledged member of the Israelite community. According to the Talmud, the practical implication of this is that should the convert revert after conversion, and then later marry an Israelite woman, it is considered a valid marriage, and not the marriage of a Jew to a non-Jew which would be invalid. Later legal authorities in Judaism have further developed this point lest it be thought that an obviously fraudulent conversion carries with it the irretrievable imprimatur of Jewishness. If the convert's acceptance was obviously an act of deception, the conversion is not valid. The Talmud speaks of a valid conversion where later on there was a reversion. The conversion was made unconditionally, as per the legal requirement. Any later change is the same as a Jew-by-birth renouncing Judaism. Whether it be a natural or naturalized Jew, the renouncing of Judaism does not change the fact of the renouncer's Jewishness.

AUTHENTICITY

How, it may be asked, is the deceit in conversion ever obvious or measurable? Since conversion involves acceptance of the monotheistic ideal, as well as adherence to the commandments spelled out in the Torah and further developed in the Talmud and codified in the Jewish legal corpus known as Shulhan Arukh, if the convert should, for example, immediately after towelling off from the ritual immersion, have a breakfast of ham and eggs, it would be obvious that the conversion was fraudulent.

It may be argued that the perfunctory adherence to commandments as a ritualistic exercise is not an indication of sincerity. However, it is always difficult to probe the deeper recesses of an individual's feelings to find out what is really meant. A Rabbinical court can do no more than go by the expressed avowals of faith and commitment and the ensuing consistent actions. If not, conversion itself becomes reduced to an exercise of deeper analysis which very few are capable of mastering, or it becomes subject to the constant espionage of an already suspicious elite.

The sincerity of the convert is a crucial issue in the conversion process. Sincerity, as the most necessary quality linked to the tangible acceptance of concrete precepts, is the primary concern of the Rabbinical court. The Talmud seems to indicate that conversion need not take more than a few minutes. The candidate for conversion comes, is discouraged three times and, if persistent, is accepted as sincere, instructed in some of the basics, circumcized, and then after the circumcision heals, ritually immersed to finalize the conversion. For the female, who need not go through circumcision, the entire procedure could theoretically take no more than one hour. Yet, any Rabbinical court which would make a practice of such instant conversions would be pilloried by the Jewish community.

One famous convert writes that he was stretched out for a period of five years before the rabbinical court in London, England accepted him (Carmel, 1967, pp. 111-112). Different courts use different methods of dissuasion, but ultimately none have the right to close the door. In fact, it is not the Rabbinical court which converts. Rather, it is the convert who converts. The Rabbinical court is no more than a catalytic agent ensuring that the requirements of conversion are satisfied. The onus is upon the convert to prove readiness, but once this is proven, the Rabbinical court is obliged to finalize the conversion procedure. Being ready to convert is not an easily achieved state. In Talmudic times, when it was hardly advantageous to be Jewish, one could almost implicitly sense the sincerity of a prospect. Similarly, a German soldier in the Warsaw Ghetto who would opt for conversion would not have his sincerity doubted, although he would undoubtedly have to pass a sanity test.

DETACHMENT - ATTACHMENT

Conversion involves a process of detachment and then a process of attachment. There must be a detachment from idolatry, pagan roots, and any theology inconsistent with Judaism, followed by attachment to Jewish beliefs and practice. However, as has been observed, aside from outstanding exceptions, it will generally be found that those who are prepared to change their religion neither had a deep religious allegiance before the change nor will have one after the change (Jakobovits, 1977, p. 213). Those with firm religious convictions find it most difficult to move away from those convictions.

The most specific problem in this area evolves around the belief in Jesus, which is totally unacceptable in Jewish theology and which a prospective convert finds very difficult to give up. Thus,

> To effect a total religious commitment which is to endure for a lifetime, and for children beyond, more than a declaration of intent is required. It is brought about by radical changes inside the person's heart determining all his future loyalties, his thinking, feelings and actions, and the mold of his very personality, in many respects even more bindingly and incisively than the commitment involved in a bond of marriage or in the adoption of a child. *A conversion, in the Jewish view, is the most delicate heart operation to which a person could ever submit.* (Jakobovits, 1977, p. 211)

Judaism does not feel constrained to admit prospective converts just because they have expressed an interest or desire to become Jewish. Judaism has never posited that salvation is dependent upon being Jewish. In fact, the Judaic view is that to be eligible for the future world all people must only observe the basic seven Noachide laws. Being Jewish involves 613 commandments, or a burden of an extra 606 commandments. Why inflict the burden?

Only if the convert is willing to accept all of the comandments is he or she accepted. The convert cannot say, "I accept all except one commandment or one nuance" (Talmud, *Bekhorot*, 30b; Maimonides, Mishnah Torah, *Laws of Forbidden Intercourse*, 14:8). The convert must accept Judaism on Judaism's terms, free from personal whim.

On the other hand, the Rabbinical court is not responsible for teaching all of the 613 commandments or, even within the basic commandments, to burden the convert with all of the details and minutia of the specific precepts.

OPEN BUT RESERVED

Judaism accepts all prospective converts "as people," but admittedly sets high standards for acceptance "as Jews." This indicates less of an interest in Judaism's numerical strength than an interest in sincere commitment, combined with wariness about diluting Judaic commitment.

It is a well-known fact that most candidates for conversion today come because they have "fallen in love with a Jewish partner." A fair guess is that upwards of 95% of all conversions are precipitated by this circumstance. Factually, only about 25% of non-Jewish girls marrying Jewish males convert, and only a fractional percentage of non-Jewish males marrying Jewish girls convert (Massarik, no date). There are many reasons for this seeming disparity, the most noteworthy of which are that conversion for a male is much more complicated since it involves circumcision. Also, the stakes are not that crucial for a male conversion since the offspring of any family always have the status of the mother. If the mother is Jewish, the children are Jewish, even if the father is not; if the mother is non-Jewish, the children are non-Jewish, even if the father is Jewish. Hence, more pressure is likely to be exerted on a non-Jewish girl to convert to ensure Judaic posterity, than on a non-Jewish male, whose conversion is not deemed that essential.

Ironically, in what must be seen as a sad commentary on Judaism's self-image, the community often more readily accepts a convert whose conversion is motivated by marital considerations than a convert who converts because of love of Judaism. The Jew, burdened by a history of oppression and depressed by the constant vilification of Israel and thus, by implication, the Jews, probably questions the normalcy of anyone who would want to become Jewish for no tangible reason.

Nevertheless, Carmel's observation that the difficulty in convincing the Rabbinical court of one's sincerity is minimal when compared with the difficulty in gaining the acceptance of the larger community, still pertains (1967, p. 113). The convert still is looked upon suspiciously, is ever considered the intruder, and has a hard time becoming accepted on an equal basis, even if the convert's level of observance is superior. After all, one way of excusing one's lack of observance is to cast aspersions and doubts about the character of those who embarrassingly observe what you are obliged to observe, but have rejected.

A CONTROVERSIAL MATTER

Marriage, as a motive for conversion, is an area of great controversy. Thus,

> The ultimate test is certainly not the applicant's love for the Jewish party he or she seeks to marry. On the contrary, such an ulterior motive will militate against accepting the application. The criterion is the love of *Judaism* generated by such thorough familiarity and fascination with the Jewish way of life as to render all sacrifices, obstacles and delays worthwhile. Only if this love of Judaism, in theory and practice, transcends any other love and loyalty are the conditions for admission truly fulfilled. (Jakobovits, 1977, p. 211)

This approach is certainly not a unanimous view, even within the Orthodox tradition. There are those who argue in

176

favour of conversions for marriage to prevent losses to the Jewish fold, and to free the couple from the prohibition of intermarriage. Even if the convert, indeed the couple, will not be observant, leaving the faith is worse; accepting the convert is a religious fulfillment (Angel, 1972).

The matter remains an issue of continuing controversy. However, even if one accepts conversion for marriage as legally valid (Talmud, *Yevamot*, 24b; Shulhan Arukh, Yoreh Deah, 268:12), the question of its desirability, from a psychological point of view, demands further exploration.

Is it at any point desirable for any individual to undergo a wholesale change of commitment for the sake of marriage? The answer, in general terms, is that where the change is a desirable change, it probably is advantageous. Thus, a convicted felon, who reforms his ways so that the girl he loves will marry him, and then becomes an outstanding citizen and a worthy contributor to society at large, exemplifies a desirable change. The metamorphasized individual has a greater sense of meaning and purpose, and an increasing love for the catalyst who forced this change, namely his wife.

If the change is a burden, then one is initially likely to endure burdens in order to gain the object of immediate love. But such intensity of love is likely to wane with the passage of years at the same time as the burden of "forced commitment" is likely to increase. When the negative emotions from forced observance begin to overpower the positive emotions of love, the relationship can explode, the marriage may disintegrate, and the children, if there are any, become casualties of a superficial conversion process. In retrospect, such a couple would have been better off never marrying in the first place.

What then should be the attitude of the Rabbinical court, or more specifically, the supervising Rabbi, in most conversion instances involving marriage? In simple terms, the Rabbi confronted with a marriage-motivated conversion must divorce the marriage from the conversion. The marriage must be isolated out as a *precipating* factor in the contemplation of conversion and not as a *causal* factor for the conversion per se. In other words, the Rabbi's stance should be, "I know why you have come and it could be either a book you have read, an experience you went through, or a person you love. This now is irrelevant."

In previous generations, when conversion was condensed into a short time frame, perhaps just an hour or two, the fact of marriage as major motivation was an acute problem. Today, with the conversion procedure stretched out to about a year's duration, if not more, the marriage factor can be isolated and neutralized over time. There need be no pressure instantly to reject the prospective convert, since there is enough time available to establish sincerity. This is a crucial point that has been lost on many a Rabbi.

The entire conversion process, entered into with free-will by the prospective convert, should involve exposure to all dimensions of Jewish knowledge and possibilities for actualizing Jewish experiences on a trial basis.

THE CRUCIAL POINT

In any successful conversion, there comes a point when the convert ceases to be an outsider looking in and, instead, begins to visualize the self as a potential insider. When the candidate starts chomping at the bit, fully aware of the implications of becoming Jewish, and is uncontrollably desirous of making the leap, the time for conversion has arrived.

But in this process, the phenomenological divorce must be everpresent. The candidate should be asked and ask the self, "what if the marriage would be called off, would you still go ahead?" It is important, for the viability of the conversion, that the answer to this question be "yes" - difficult though it may seem. It establishes that the convert is not making a burdensome change only to please the partner, but is converting out of unconditional love of a newly discovered faith system. That unconditional love, divorced from the marriage situation, ensures that the convert will not ape one faith system while being emotionally attached to another, or perhaps being attached to no system whatsoever.

On balance, what appears to be a very strict and demanding approach to conversion is at the same time a psychological safeguard against haphazard changes for which many individuals are not psychologically, never mind spiritually, ready. This also helps the convert accept his or her self and the coherence of the momentous change, and thus enhances the prospects of linking with the community.

An Italian traveller in 1735 recorded in his diary the following:

> I saw...two Protestants become Jews and be circumcized, and two ladies likewise embrace the Jewish religion with great devotion. The difficulties that the Jews themselves place in the way of those who wish to become Jews are so great that it would seem impossible that anyone should resolve to take such a step. But when it is resolved, it is not taken for an ulterior motive, but because they believe that infallibly they are doing rightly. After all the warnings to proselytes, when nothing remains but the act of circumcision, and the operation is to be performed, they bring out a great knife like that with which the Jews slaughter cattle, which would put fear in a giant, shining like crystal, then the brave fellows resign themselves to endure the pain in order to embrace the Hebrew religion and to believe in the Hebrew Law as the true Law. (Shaftesley, quoted in Jakobovits, 1977, p. 212)

The great knife is, no doubt, an exaggeration. Circumcision is not a hatchet job. However, the awesomeness of conversion, perhaps, should not be an exaggeration. Rather than jump to a solution (instant conversion) which satisfies the immediate moment, it is more worthwhile to draw out the process to guarantee, as much as possible, that long range realities will be better served.

The fact that today's conversions, in many Rabbinical courts, are stretched far beyond the time element suggested in the Talmud, undoubtedly reflects hesitancies about candidate sincerity and ability to carry out commitment. However, from a psychological perspective, this very delay may be just the right medicine for an impatient prospective proselyte.

CHAPTER 12

PSYCHOANALYZING THE NAZIS

Judging by the thanatological literature which has glutted the scene in recent years, it appears that our society is having great difficulty coming to grips with death. The meaning of death, the problem of one's finite existence, the guilts associated with death and dying, are just part of the many complexities which modern society is facing with increasing dis-ease.

In this context, massive extermination and devastating Holocaust are realities which defy explanation and which even challenge one's sanity. Indeed, though we are moving further and further away from the Nazi Holocaust, the literature concerning it is proliferating. Perhaps it is only after the detachment of a few decades that one can reflect upon this most heinous deviation from humanness with some form of objectivity. Perhaps, too, it is the very passage of time and the ensuing lapses of memory which force theologians, political scientists, and psychologists to bring the past back into real life.

Serious as well as would-be theologians who address themselves to the Holocaust are mainly concerned with God's role in it and the meaning of the Holocaust in the context of Jewish history.

REUVEN P. BULKA

Political scientists tend to analyze the political side of the Holocaust, how and why powerful nations failed to intervene. Psychologists, of course, focus on the criminals and their bestiality. A common denominator of those multi-dimensional quests is the matter of guilt. Who is guilty and who is the villain of this, the blackest period of human history?

THE GUILTY

In attempting to pinpoint the guilt from a purely legal and psychological point of view, the bureaucratic notion of "the buck stops here" has been applied. Nazi criminals at Nuremberg claimed they were only following orders, that they were not to blame. The guilt, in their view, had to be placed squarely on the shoulders of one person, the architect of this massive destruction, Hitler himself.

In fact, the very process of condensing the guilt by personifying one individual as the archvillain is very much a part of people's make-up. It is part of an identification process. A country is identified through its leader, a football team through its quarterback or coach. It is convenient and, in a sense, necessary to have a personification of guilt for the Holocaust because it had to start from somewhere and someone must bear the ultimate responsibility, even though the cohorts and the so-called followers cannot escape guilt for what is obviously a crime which goes against every single moral, ethical and human fibre that an individual possesses.

But, there are dangers. The very process of reducing this massive guilt for the animal-like annihilation of six million Jews invites an escape clause. The "buck" stops at the desk of the architect and, after having spent one's psychic energy in venting one's anger at that one person, a reverse process may interfere.

It was not too long ago that a so-called historian in England claimed that Hitler himself knew nothing about what was going on in the concentration camps and was oblivious to the mass extermination taking place. This pseudo-historian based his conclusion on the "fact" that there is no evidence that Hitler knew what was taking place. This reasoning is part of a despicable system whereby, at first, all the guilt is hurled upon one person. Then that one person is exonerated for whatever obviously fraudulent rea-

182

sons, such that there was no crime because there were no criminals. If anything, it is the air which is to blame. The next step, of course, would be the victimology syndrome whereby the Holocaust will be viewed as a plague visited upon the Jews spontaneously. The Jews found their way into the crematoria on their own; the Jews themselves brought on their destruction!

For this reason, one should welcome the continuing scientific investigation into the minds of the Nazi leaders of the 1930s and 1940s. Even if these studies might not reach legitimate conclusions, nevertheless, they keep ever-present in our minds the tragedy of the past and, serve to prevent its recurrence. This appreciation, however, must not mute a sober, analytic critique of the studies presented.

WERE THEY NORMAL?

Two authors, Florence A. Miale, a psychotherapist and Rorschach specialist, and Michael Selzer, a political scientist, probe the psyche of the Nazi leaders (1975). They ask: were the Nazi leaders normal people? The question is a vital one in terms of pinpointing with precision where the guilt rests. Ostensibly, we would tend to associate guilt with normality; that is, only those individuals who would be judged as sane could be considered responsible, and therefore guilty.

Hannah Arendt's theory of the banality of evil is quite well known. Eichmann, she says, could perform any task without regard to its moral nature and no matter how cruel, following the true spirit of obedience to others. He was a normal, ordinary person in Arendt's view. Miale and Selzer sharply attack Arendt's view. They claim that the very inability to differentiate between good and evil and, instead,to hide behind the imperative for obedience, speaks of psychological aberrance. They also jump on Arendt's assertion concerning Eichman being an average, normal person, as testified to by six psychiatrists, one psychiatrist even saying that Eichmann was more normal than he. (The cynic might feel that such an observation is not saying much.) These informal views, say the authors, are really not admissible, especially in the light of tests analyzed by Dr. Szondi who, not knowing who the subject was, said that the person (Eichmann) whose tests he saw indicated a man obsessed with a dangerous and insatiable urge to kill...a perverted, sadistic personality.

The authors also cite the famous experiments of Stanley Milgram who took many subjects and placed them in front of a shock generator with thirty switches ranging in voltage from 15 to 450 and labelled from "slight shock" to "danger-severe shock." Those who administered the shocks were the teachers. Those to whom the shocks were administered were the learners. Any mistake by the learners was reason to administer the shock as punishment. At 75 volts, the learner grunted, at 120 volts, the learner complained bitterly, at 150 volts, the learner demanded release, and at 285 volts, the learner would scream agonizingly. Lest the reader think Milgram to be a sadistic maniac, it should be stated that the learners really did not receive the shocks, but only simulated receiving them. They were good actors.

The behaviour of the teachers in punishing each mistake of the learner with a shock was monitored by an "experimenter" who would urge the teacher to administer the shock with statements such as "please continue" or the authoritative "you have no other choice, you must go on."

Though they sometimes sweated, trembled, and showed other forms of reluctance, 65 percent of the "teachers" obeyed orders all the way to the end of the scale of the shock generator. Not a single teacher disobeyed the orders to continue before 300 volts, which was marked "intense shock," and then only 12 1/2 percent stopped.

Milgram made some variations in the experiment. It turned out that when the teachers were told by the experimenters to use their own judgement but to continue to administer shock, and were then left alone, the level of shock administered dropped considerably. It dropped most dramatically when the teachers were allowed to select the shock level themselves. The level then was reduced to 55 volts, or "slight shock." Milgram found that the teachers were not even upset. He theorizes that the teachers, in fact, had placed the responsibility for their actions on the shoulders of the experimenters.

The connection between Milgram's experiment and the Nazi leaders is obvious. There appears to be a natural propensity amongst people to follow orders, no matter how inhumane those orders may be. The Nazis, as far as Milgram is concerned, were not the exception, they were the norm.

Miale and Selzer legitimately question the validity of Milgram's conclusions. They claim that Milgram's experiment fails to tackle the real problem, which is the perennial chicken/egg dilemma. Was it the orders which gave birth to the aggression or was it the aggression which allowed the orders to be followed? Miale and Selzer make a good case for the point that obedient subjects had a different set of values and that the command of the experimenter to administer the shocks *"gave sanction to and released the aggressive drives of the so-called obedient subjects"* (1975, p. 11). The experimenter gave those with aggressive drives an opportunity to express that very aggression.

The authors buffer their point with the finding by Kohlberg that those who broke off from administering shock were at a higher level of moral development than those who remained obedient to the end, a finding which Milgram conveniently explains away.

So, for Miale and Selzer, the question is still open. One can already sense from the way they attack the views of Arendt and Milgram that they will come up with a different proposition. Indeed, their conclusion, following an intense investigation of the personalities of sixteen Nazi leaders, is that "The Nazis were not psychologically normal or healthy individuals" (p. 287). This conclusion is based on Rorschach tests administered to sixteen leading Nazis, including Hans Frank, Hermann Goering, Rudolf Hess, Constantin von Neurath, Joachim von Ribbentrop, Baldur von Schirach and Albert Speer, while these beasts were awaiting trial.

THE TEST

A Rorschach assessment is based on a series of ten images (ink blots), which a subject is asked to view. Herman Rorschach, the Swiss psychiatrist who designed this test, felt that the objects which were seen by the subject in the ink blots were not randomly perceived, but rather based on the individual's distinctive characteristics, which could be identified through the response. A Rorschach analysis is very sensitive and must be made objectively. Miale and Selzer indicate that the Rorschach record of Goering was shown to a small group of Rorschach experts informally. The identity of the subject was not revealed, yet the psychologists recognized the pattern as one of a dangerous psychopathic person. However, the general pattern is that Rorschach records are not looked at "blindly," or so the authors claim. They readily admit (p. 28) that they made their analyses of these sixteen Rorschach patterns with an awareness that they were dealing with Nazis and even with an awareness of details of their individual lives. Miale and Selzer claim, however, that this does not undermine the validity of their assessments.

However, Richard Rubenstein, in reviewing this book, refuses to accept that the authors made an objective study (Rubenstein, 1976, pp. 83-84). Not only were they aware of their subjects, they also did not use some form of control group of other elites to find out whether the Nazi responses were significantly different from people in comparable positions in other communities.

To show how delicate an instrument the Rorschach test is, consider the different conclusions with regard to the Nazis which were reached independently by Miale and Selzer on the one hand, and Molly Harrower on the other (Harrower, 1976, pp. 76-80). Miale and Selzer found, on a general level, that fifteen of the sixteen subjects indicated a depressive mood, were underdeveloped, manipulative and hostile, rejected responsibility, and were generally psychopathic. Harrower, in fact, submitted eight Rorschachs, seven of which were the same used by Miale and Selzer, to ten acknowledged authorities in Rorschach interpretation. She categorized the eight into four separate categories:
(1) superior personalities - Schacht and von Schirach
(2) normal personalities - Eichmann and Goering
(3) less than adequate personalities - Hess and von Neurath
(4) disturbed or impoverished personalities - von Ribbentrop and Speer

In the superior and normal personality categories, Harrower also included for analysis the Rorschach records of a clergyman-civil rights leader and an improved psychiatric patient. Nine out of the ten judges thought that the superior records were all similar; six thought that they were all superior adults, two thought they were civil rights leaders and one thought they were psychologists (normal ones, I assume).

In a different pattern reflecting the backgrounds of the test-takers, two groups of Nazis, four in each group, a separate group of four clergymen and a group of four test records from two patients, one set when each was disturbed and one set when each was improved, were submitted. The experts did not feel that the groupings had anything in common but some saw a similarity in the first group of Nazis. One thought they were a cross section of middle-class Americans. Another thought they were well-known superior adults, while another thought they were military men, but not war criminals. One of the experts saw a similarity in the second group of Nazis, but thought they could be members of the clergy!

The gap between the findings of Miale and Selzer and those done by the blind studies of Harrower is stupendous. It makes one wonder where is the truth. This should convince the reader that Rorschach analysis is no simple matter and that if anything, the method of analyzing the Rorschach records used by Miale and Selzer who were fully aware of the subjects they were analyzing, leaves their conclusions open to question.

QUESTIONABLE OBSERVATIONS

Miale and Selzer, however well-intentioned, engage in some very questionable tactics in their analyses of the Rorschach. A few examples will illustrate the point. Concerning Alfred Rosenberg, who was involved in the brutalities of extermination, they write:

The Nazi doctrines that Rosenberg would at a somewhat later stage in his life begin to articulate rather clearly reveal his attempt to use a political restructuring of the world as a compensation for his own, inner lack of structure. (p. 194)

Why accuse the poor fellow of destroying when, in fact, he was trying to build!

Of Arthur Seyss-Inquart, who was found to be ruthless in applying terrorism to suppress all opposition to the German occupation, the authors state:

> At least part of his propensity for, and experience of, violence and destruction had its origin in a deep sense of homelessness and rootlessness. (p. 253)

Why blame the poor fellow for all of his violence, when it really is his lack of a home which should be blamed!

More diasppointing is the author's analysis of Goering, of whom it was said by the judges of Nuremberg that "his guilt is unique in its enormity. The record discloses no excuses for this man." But Miale and Selzer offer excuses. Goering's mother, we are told, left him a few weeks after his birth to return to her husband in Haiti. Goering was raised by a family friend. His earliest recollection of meeting his mother was upon her return from Haiti. As she bent down to embrace him, he hit her in the face with both fists (p. 96).

> The Rorschach record points up the more profound and lasting effects of Goering's childhood experience. The maternal deprivation he suffered as a small child engendered sufficient anger, as we have seen, to cause him to hit his mother in the face when he was reunited with her: significantly, this was Goering's earliest memory. Some of the violence and depression in his Rorschach record surely has its origins in this experience of deprivation and so too, we may be sure, does some of the great depression within him. One of the most striking aspects of his Rorschach is the evidence of his extreme inability to respond to nuances of feeling in human relationships.... This inability, too, surely has its origins in his experience of maternal deprivation as a small child. (p. 97)

Continuing along those lines, the authors point out that Goering's mother was the mistress of a Dr. von Epenstein, a wealthy Jewish apostate. This apostate bought a splendid home for the elder Goerings, but even there, a special bedroom was reserved for Epenstein and his lover, and the elder Goering was not allowed to enter these rooms. Instead, he was forced to sleep in a modest bedroom on the ground floor. Miale and Selzer try to show that the Rorschach indicates how Hermann Goering felt he was being cut open by the conflict between Epenstein and his own father; thus, Goering would feel violent towards Epenstein. And, the *coup de grace*:

> It hardly requires saying that Goering's anti-Semitism must have been rooted, in large part, in the knowledge that Epenstein was a Jew. (p. 98)

These are just a few examples of a trend which is found throughout the book. At no point do the authors indicate that their psychoanalysis of the Nazi leaders is an attempt to get them off the hook. But, willy-nilly, this is precisely what they achieve! After all, the unsuspecting reader who reads the analysis of Hermann Goering, if that reader has any sensitivity, would almost be led to tears of sympathy for this poor beast. Not only is his violence explained away through the Rorschach, but also his vicious anti-Semitism. Not only does it all make sense, it is even given the stamp of legitimacy because the causality is logical and the consequence is a natural result of past experience.

The authors admit that their analysis does not explain the rise of Nazism, but the rise of Nazism cannot be understood without a proper understanding of these leaders. Their explication is part of the explanation.

The Nazis, generally speaking, are branded by Miale and Selzer as psychopaths. The psychopath often has a father or grandfather who is prominently respected, such as a judge, a civic leader, or a clergyman (rabbis, beware). The father is stern, remote, obsessional; the mother is indulgent, pleasure-loving and contemptuous of her husband's importance. The parents usually display dependence on the approval of their contemporaries. The relationship between parent and child is poor from the early stages, and instead of real love, one is likely to find indulgence and solicitude. There is an emphasis on external appearances. The child must behave well in order to reflect favourably on the parents. Miale and Selzer tell us that the Rorschach records of the Nazis "strongly suggest that their early years and their family life were characterized by the kind of dynamics" which led to the formation of the psychopathic personality (p. 281).

REUVEN P. BULKA

DUBIOUS FAVOUR

It is wrong to accuse the authors of blantantly trying to excuse the Nazis. In fact, it is obvious from the way they write that they feel they are doing the world a favour by showing that the Nazis were not normal. Whether this is indeed a favour is another matter.

Firstly, such explaining away tends to lull the contemporary world into a false sense of security with the thought that we will never again have such a conglomeration of psychopaths. Not only is the hope that we will never have such a psychopathic conglomerate unrealistic, but the question of whether the Nazis were indeed psychopathic is itself still debatable.

Secondly, branding the Nazis as psychopathic, all good intentions to the contrary, tends to absolve legally these two-legged animals of their guilt. After all, how can you blame a psychopath for psychopathic behaviour when that psychopathic behaviour is an accident of the individual's psychopathology? This is not explicitly stated by Miale and Selzer, nor do they hint at it, but the very fact that they project their analysis in this direction, with such finality, begs this crucial point. The one who gave the orders was not normal, those who obeyed and carried out the orders were not normal, the whole situation was abnormal, so legally, there was no crime. Therefore, there was no guilt.

Miale and Selzer have, at best, composed a questionable piece of scientific literature. At worst, they have projected a fraudulent but potent argument for releasing the Nazis from guilt. All the anticipation which greets a study of the Nazis is dissolved into profound disappointment upon realization that this study is a potentially dangerous piece of work.

To be sure, Miale and Selzer are not the only ones who psychoanalyze away the guilt of the Nazis. Consider the following:

The insecurities of post-World War I Germany and the anxieties they produced provided an emotional milieu in which irrationality and hysteria became routine and illusions became transformed into delusions. The delusional

190

disorder assumed mass proportions. Germans, otherwise individually rational, yielded themselves to pathological fantasies about the Jews. In that climate, where masses of Germans had lost the ability to distinguish between the real Jew and the mythic Jew of anti-Semitic invention, the chiliastic system of National Socialist beliefs could further their already distorted sense of reality...in modern Germany, the mass psychosis of anti-Semitism deranged a whole people. (Davidowitz, 1975, pp. 164-165)

Introducing such notions as "mass psychosis" serves to denormalize the Nazis and thus tends to absolve them. It is to be hoped that Davidowitz used the term "mass psychosis" not as a clinical or moral judgment, but as a form of hyperbole to which she may be entitled by literary license. Nevertheless, the dangers of using such terms indiscriminately are too massive to allow such license.

FREE-CHOICE

Where, indeed, do we stand on the problem of Nazi guilt? What they did could not have been normal because no normal human being would perpetrate such atrocities. If, indeed, what they did was not normal and they were psychopathic, then there was no free-willed action. One recalls the differing analyses of the Rorschach offered by Miale and Selzer and the ten experts consulted by Harrower. The objective analyses of Harrower's experts were radically different from the analyses of Miale and Selzer, but they were the same Rorschachs. One can see a multitude of attributes and tendencies in the same person. Does this not indicate that, in fact, every individual has a multitude of propensities and potentialities ranging all the way from docility to violence, from mercifulness to cruelty, from cold insensitivity to warm empathy? Is it the propensity which makes the individual or is it the individual who makes the propensity into a reality?

The Talmud asserts that a person is led on the course he or she wishes to follow (*Makkot*, 10b). That is to say, the choices make the person. Even if one were to assume that individuals are born with basic tendencies, these tendencies do not imply causality. After all, does not the Talmud assert that "One who is born under the constellation of Mars will be a shedder of blood." Lest the student think that this concept contradicts the basic Judaic notion of free choice, Rav Ashi intervenes and explains, "either a surgeon, a thief, a slaughterer or a circumciser" (*Shabbat*, 156a). The world is varied enough that even tendencies towards violence can be given positive expression and release. That one chooses to release these tendencies in an abominable manner becomes a matter of choice. There are many children of famous personalities — not all of them become psychopaths; there are many children who are denied maternal love — not all of them become insensitive, cruel killers; there are many children who see conflict in their homes — not all of them become violent. Deprivation limits choices, but it does not destroy choice. Even when reflecting upon the plight of Pharaoh, who was the agent of God's destiny in enslaving the Jewish people in Egypt, Jewish philosophers excuse Pharaoh from blame for the actual enslavement, since this was really part of God's plan, for which he was a mere agent. It was the cruel subjugation and unnecessary murders of innocents for which Pharaoh was blamed. Pharaoh's culpability derived from his own, freely-willed "contribution" of cruelty. Destiny was involved, but so was free choice.

The syndrome of enslavement is separate from the syndrome of murder (this is not to imply that enslavement is an acceptable enterprise). It is the human refusal to exercise humanness which makes the one follow the other. This was the case with Pharaoh and this was the case with the Nazis. Their guilt is the guilt of human beings who freely chose to become animals.

Miale and Selzer, in their introduction, dedicate their book to the victims of the Nazis, living and dead. Immediately underneath is the Hebrew verse, *"Zakhor et asher asah l'kha Amalek,"* "Rembmer what Amalek did unto you" (*Deuteronomy*, 25:17). The Scripture continues with the fact that Amalek made an inexcusable and wanton attack on the Jewish people just for the sake of eliminating them. Because of this, the Jewish community is charged with the obligation to *"blot out* the memory of Amalek" (*Deuteronomy*, 25:19).

It should be noted that the Rorschach test is referred to as the "ink blot" test. Obviously the authors, Miale and Selzer, felt that by subjecting the Nazis to "ink blot" analysis, they were "blotting out" the memory of modern day Amalek, but, in fact, what they have achieved is to blot out their guilt. Insofar as this was not the intention of the authors, it is unfortunate. Insofar as this gives added ammunition to those who desire to absolve the Nazis from any blame, it is disastrous.

CONCLUDING THOUGHTS

One issue, above all others, has today grabbed center stage — the nuclear arms race. Economic, moral, and bio-ethical concerns are still debated, but we are all aware that if the nuclear arms confrontation escalates into war, all other issues will become irrelevant. Mass and massive death will pervade life.

While there are those who would rush to declare *a*, or even *the* Jewish attitude to nuclear arms control, such bandwagoning is really unnecessary. A value system so committed to life, in quantity and quality, as Judaism is, could be nothing less than vehemently opposed to nuclear proliferation. But, to abuse an old phrase, it takes two to un-tango, at least in this issue. Push as we must to defuse the nuclear time bomb, it must come from an immediate and total awareness that nuclear confrontation involves two parties, two factions, two forces. If peace and harmony, free from nuclear anxiety is the goal, it should be realized in the framework of the Hebrew word for peace, shalom. Shalom means peace, it means harmony, but it also connotes equality, fairness, balance, completeness. All these are necessary components in a nuclear de-escalation as the first step in the messianic hope for a demilitarized world which solves its problems with words and books, rather than guns and bombs.

In such a world, debating the issues raised in this volume can only add meaning and value to humanity in search of itself.

195

GLOSSARY

Abravanel - commentator on the Bible
aggadah - Judaic homiletical literature
atzmo - one's self
averah lishmah - transgression performed with good intentions
avodah zarah - idolatry
baal teshuvah - penitent
bat kol - heavenly voice
bayn adam lahavero - between the individual and the
                individual's friend
bayn adam LaMakom - between the individual and the Creator
Beit Hamidrash - house of study
ben - son of
Bet Hillel - School of Hillel
Bet Shammai - School of Shammai
birkhat kohanim - priestly blessing
brakhah - blessing
cubit - about 18 inches
epikores - non-believer, scoffer
haggadah - basic text of the main passover celebration, called
        "Seder"
halakhah - Jewish law applied to life
halakhic - of, or pertaining to the halakhah
hallah - priestly portion of the dough
Hananya, Mishael & Azarya - Jewish heroes of yesteryear
hasid - member of hasidic sect, adhering to the specific norms
      and customs   of that group
hasid shoteh - foolish pietist
hasidic - pertaining to the Hasidim
Hasidim - members of hasidic sect adhering to hasidic philosophy and norms
havurot - intimate groups who share Jewish experiences
        together as a family
hazzan - cantor, community leader in prayer
hidur mitzvah - beautifying the commandment
Hillel - Talmudic sage
hivuv mitzvah - love of commandment
hupah - wedding canopy
Kadesh - stop on Israel's route from Egypt to the promised land
kallah - bride

karet - premature death
kashrut - pertaining to maintaining kosher regulations
kavanah - single mindedness, concentration in fulfilling
          precepts
ketuvah - marriage contract
kiddushim - repasts following Shabbat services
kohen - priest
kosher - conforming to the ritual rules of Jewish law and thus fit
          to be eaten
lazet yedei shamayim - to fulfill the dicates of heaven
Levi - one of the twelve tribes of Israel
levites - members of the levitic tribe
lifnim meshurat hadin - within the boundary of the law
lishmah - proper intent for fulfilling precepts
l'maan telekh b'derekh tovim - that you walk in the way of
                                good people
lulav - palm branch, part of the ritual of the Tabernacles Festival
Magen Avraham - commentary on code of Jewish law
Maharsha - talmudic commentary
Maimonides - Jewish philosopher and legalist of 12th century
matzah - unleavened bread, the staple for Passover
me'abed atzmo lada'at - destroying oneself wittingly
menuhah - contentedness
midot hasidut - the way of the pious
midrash - homiletic exegesis of the Bible
mikvah - ritual bath for immersion to attain purity
mishnah - legal formulations forming the basic text enlarged
           upon in the Gemara, the two together making up
           what is referred to as the Talmud
Mishnah Torah - classic codification of the Talmud, by
                 Maimonides
mitnaged - singular of mitnagdim
mitnagdim - opposers of Hasidism
mitzvah - biblical commandment
mitzvot - plural of mitzvah
Moshe Rabbenu - Hebrew title for Moses (literally, Moses our
                 master teacher)
musar - reproof
Nahmanides - thirteenth century sage and commentator
nasi - president
nesiat kappayim - recitation of the priestly blessing

Nitzavim - one of the last sections of the Bible, containing last
charges of Moses to the Israelites
Noachide laws - seven regulations of basic morality and ethics
Orah Hayyim - one of the sections of Code of Jewish Law
Passover - festival celebrating Israelites' gaining freedom from
slavery
Poskim - halakhic (legal) authorities
RAbad - adversarial commentary to Maimonides
RaN - commentary on the Talmud
Rashi - classic commentator on the Bible and Talmud
Refidim - stop on Israel's route from Egypt to the promised
land
Rosh Hashanah - first day of the year, spent in meditation and
prayer
Rosh Hodesh - first day of the month
Sefer Hahinukh - thirteenth century work expanding on the 613
commandments
Shabbat - Jewish day of rest, comprising the period between
sundown Friday and after sunset on Saturday
shabbos-dik - consistent with the rules and spirit of Shabbat
shamor - keep, referring to avoidance of that which is
prohibited
Shavuot - festival celebrating the receipt of the Torah at Mount
Sinai
sheva brakhot - seven blessings recited at a wedding
shidukh - matching person with mate
shidukhim - plural of shidukh
sh'ma - classic Jewish affirmation of faith recited twice daily
shofar - ram's horn sounded on Rosh Hashanah
shoteh - one who is behaviourally deficient
shtetl - old world term conveying the idea of a city or
community with warmth
shul - another term for synagogue
Shulhan Arukh - Code of Jewish Law
Sukkot - tabernacle festival
synagogue - Jewish house of prayer
tallit - prayer shawl
Talmud - explication of the Bible, translating biblical
imperatives into everyday norms
TaZ - commentary on Code of Jewish law
teshuvah - repentance

Torah - corpus of Jewish law and lore, incorporating Bible,
    Talmud, Midrash, commentary, and responsa
Tosafot - commentary on the Talmud
v'anvayhu - adorning the precepts
v'aseeta hayashar v'hatov - you shall do that which is right
    and good
Vayelekh - one of the last sections of the Bible, describing
    Moses' last actions
yeshiva - Jewish grade school accenting Talmudic studies
yeshivot - plural of yeshiva
Yom Kippur - day of atonement, spent totally in meditation and
    prayer, amidst abstinence from food
yom tov - Jewish festival
y'oosh - giving up hope for recovering a lost object
Yore Deah - one of the sections of Code of Jewish Law
zakhor - remember, referring to actualizing that which is
    mandated
zaddikim - righteous people
zerizut - eagerness to fulfill precepts
zimun - gathering together for eating, and the grace which
    follows

BIBLIOGRAPHY

Abravanel, D. *Commentary on the Torah* (3 vols.). Tel-Aviv: HapoelHamizrachi Publishing, 1964.

Albee, G. To thine own self be true. *American Psychologist*, 1975, 30, 1156-1158.

Allport, G. "Comments on earlier chapters." In Rollo May (ed.), *Existential Psychology*. New York: Random House, 1961.

— *The individual and his religion: A psychological interpretation*. New York: MacMillan, 1950.

Alvarez, A. *The savage god: A study of suicide*. Middlesex, England: Penguin Books, 1974.

Angel, M. Another halakhic approach to conversions. *Tradition*, Winter-Spring, 1972, 12(3-4), 107-113.

Appel, G. (ed.). *Samuel K. Mirsky memorial volume: Studies in Jewish law, philosophy, and literature*. New York: Yeshiva University Press, 1970.

Ashkenazi, B. *Shitah Mekubetzet* (Vol. 11). Tel-Aviv: A. Zioni Publishing, 1963.

Baer, J. *How to be an assertive (not aggressive) woman in life, in love, and on the job: A total guide to self-assertiveness*. Scarborough, Ont.: New American Library, 1976.

Bahr, S. & Day, R. Sex role attitudes, female employment and marital satisfaction. *Journal of Comparative Family Studies*, Spring 1978, 9(1), 53-67.

Baron, R. & D. Byrne. *Social psychology: Understanding human interaction*. Boston: Allyn & Bacon, 1981.

Becker, E. The Spectrum of loneliness. *Humanitas: Journal of the Institute of Man*, November 1974, 10(3), 237-246.

Beckhouse, L., J. Tanur, J. Weiler & E. Weinstein. And some men have leadership thrust upon them. *Journal of Personality and Social Psychology*, 1975, 31, 557-566.

Belkin, S. *In His Image*. New York: Abelard-Schuman, 1960.

Berkovits. *E/ *Crisis and Faith*, New York: Sanhedrin Press, 1976.

Berman, S. The status of women in halakhic Judaism. *Tradition*, Fall 1973, 14(2), 5-28.

Berry, N. Portrait of a family conservationist. *Marriage and Family Living*, October 1978, 60(10), 10-13.

Blass, J. Some personality correlates of religious orientation among Jewish seminarians. *Journal of Psychology and Judaism*, 1979, 4(2), 68-77.

Bronfenbrenner, U. Nobody home: The erosion of the American family. *Psychology Today*, May 1977, 10(12), 41-47.

Buber, M. *Tales of the hasidim: The early masters*. New York: Schocken Books, 1958.

Bulka, R. The role of the individual in Jewish law. *Tradition*, Spring-Summer 1973, 13(4) - 14(1), 123-136.

— Setting the tone: The psychology-Judaism dialogue. *Journal of Psychology and Judaism*, Fall, 1976, 1(1), 3-13.

— *The quest for ultimate meaning: Principles and applications of logotherapy*. New York: Philosophical Library, 1979.

— Statistics Canada publishes a scary tale about increasing number of intermarriages. *Family and Marraige Newsletter of the Rabbinical Council of America*, 1981, 5(3).

Camus, A. *The myth of Sisyphus*. New York: Vintage Books, 1955.

Carlin, J. & S. Mendlovitz. The American rabbi: A religious specialist responds to loss of authority. In J. Neusner (ed.), *Understanding American Judaism: Towards the description of a modern religion. Volume One - The Rabbi and the Synanogue.* New York: Ktav Publishing House & Anti-Defamation League of B'nai B'rith, 1975.

Carmel, A. The proselyte - A blessing or a curse? In P. Longworth (ed.), *Confrontations with Judaism.* London: Anthony Blond, 1967.

Chesler, P. *Women and madness.* New York: Avon Books, 1973

Cohen, A. *The myth of the Judeo-Christian tradition.* New York: Schocken Books, 1971.

Cohen, A. (ed.). *The Minor Tractates of the Talmud* (2 vols.). London: Soncino Press, 1965.

Cohen, H. Suicide in Jewish legal and religious tradition. *Mental Health and Society,* 1976, 3, 129-136.

Cunningham,. M., J. Steinberg & R. Grev. Wanting to and having to help: Separate motivations for positive mood and guilt-induced helping. *Journal of Personality and Social Psychology,* 1980, 38, 181-192.

Davidowitz, L. *The war against the Jews, 1933-1945.* New York: Holt, Reinhart and Winston, 1975.

Davids, L. Jewish marriage breakdown in Canada: Some plain facts. In R. Bulka (ed.), *Family and Marriage Newsletter of the Rabbinical Council of America,* 1981, 5(2).

Ein Yaakov, (Vol. 3). New York: Pardes Publishing Co., 1955.

Elazar, D. *Community and Polity: The organizational dynamics of American Jewry.* Philadelphia: Jewish Publication Society, 1976.

Ellis, A. *Humanistic psychotherapy: The rational-emotive approach.* New York: McGraw-Hill, 1973.

Epstein, Y. *Arukh Hahulhan* (Vol. 5). New York: Grossman Publishing, (no date).

Erikson, E. Inner and outer space: Reflections on womanhood. *Daedalus*, 1964, 93(2), 582-606.

Eysenck, H. The effects of psychotherapy: An evaluation. *Journal of Consulting Psychology*, 1952, 16, 319-324.

Farrar, C. Suicide. *Journal of Clinical and Experimental Psychopathology*, 1951, 12(1), 79-88.

The Fathers according to Rabbi Nathan (J. Goldin, trans.). New Haven:Yale University Press, 1955.

Faulkner, B. *Burnout in ministry: How to recognize it, how to avoid it*. Nashville, Tennessee: Broadman Press, 1981.

Feldman, M. Women and g'marah: Kasha or teretz. *Kol Yavneh*, December 1976-January 1977, 5(1), p. 17.

Fiedler, F. and M. Chemers. *Leadership and effective management*. Glenview, Illionis: Scott, Foresman, 1974.

Fodor, E. Simulated work climate as an influence on choice of leadership style. *Personality and Social Psychology Bulletin*, 1978, 4, 111-114.

Frankl, V. *Man's search for meaning: An introduction to logotherapy*. New York: Washington Square Press, 1963.

— Time and responsibility. *Existential Psychiatry*, 1966, 1, 361-366.

— *The doctor and the soul: From psychotherapy to logotherapy*. New York: Bantam Books, 1967.

— *Psychotherapy and existentialism. Selected papers on logotherapy*. New York: Simon and Schuster, 1968.

— *The unconscious God: Psychotherapy and theology*. New York: Simon and Schuster, 1975.

— *The unheard cry for meaning: Psychotherapy and humanism.* New York: Simon and Schuster, 1978.

Freudenberger, H. & G. Richelson. *Burnout: How to beat the high cost of success.* New York: Bantam Books, 1981.

Fromm, E. *Psychoanalysis and religion.* New Haven: Yale University Press, 1950.

— *The Forgotten Language.* New York: Grove Press, 1957.

Friedman, H. and M. Simon (eds.). *The Midrash* (10 vols.). London: Soncino Press, 1961.

Fromm-Reichman, F. Loneliness. *Psychiatry*, February 1959, 22, 1-15.

Gendler, M. Sarah's seed: A new ritual for women. *Response*, Winter 1974-1975, 24, 65-75.

Gilder, G. *Sexual suicide.* New York: Bantam Books, 1975.

Glenn, N. & C. Weaver. A multivariate, multisurvey study of mental happiness. *Journal of Marriage and the Family*, May 1978, 40(2), 269-282.

Gornick, V. & B. Moran (eds.). *Women in sexist society: Studies in power and powerlessness.* New York: New American Library, 1972.

Gotz, I. Loneliness. *Humanitas: Journal of the Institute of Man*, November 1974, 10(3), 289-299.

Greenberg, I. Comment. In J. Neusner (ed.), *Understanding American Judaism: Toward the description of a modern religion. Volume One - The Rabbi and the Synagogue.* New York: Ktav Publishing House and Anti-Defamation League of B'nai B'rith, 1975.

Greenberg, S. The Rabbinate and the Jewish community structure. In J. Neusner (ed.), *Understanding American Judaism: Toward the description of a modern religion. Volume One - The Rabbi and the Synagogue.* New York: Ktav Publishing House and Anti-Defamation League of B'nai B'rith, 1975.

Greenwald, Y. *Kol bo on mourning.* New York: Feldheim, 1965.

Gross, M.L. *The psychological society. A critical analysis of psychiatry, psychotherapy, psychoanalysis and the psychological revolution.* New York: Simon and Schuster, 1978.

Harper, R. The Concentric Circles of Loneliness. *Humanitas: Journal of the Institute of Man,* November 1974, 10(3), 247-253.

Harrower, M. Were Hitler's henchmen mad? *Psychology Today,* July 1976, 10(2), 76-80.

Hassett, J. "But that would be wrong...". *Psychology Today,* November 1981, 15(11), 34-50.

Hollander, E. & J. Julien. Studies in leader legitimacy, influence, and innovation. In L. Berkowitz (ed.), *Advances in experimental social psychology* (Vol. 5). New York: Academic Press, 1970.

The Holy Scriptures (2 Vols.). Philadelphia: Jewish Publication Society,1917.

Hora, T. Psychotherapy, existence and religion. In Hendrik M. Ruitenbeek (ed.), *Psychoanalysis and existential philosophy.* New York: E.P. Dutton, 1962.

Isen, A. & P. Levin. The effect of feeling good on helping: Cookies and kindness. *Journal of Personality and Social Psychology,* 1972, 21, 384-388.

Jakobovits, I. *The timely and the timeless: Jews, Judaism and society in a storm-tossed decade.* London: Vallentine, Mitchell, 1977.

Judah the Pious. *Sefer-Hasidim.* Jerusalem: Mosad Harav Kuk, 1970.

Kelman, W. The Synagogue in America. In J. Neusner (ed.),
*Understanding American Judaism: Toward the description of a
modern religion. Volume One - The Rabbi and the Synagogue.* New
York: Ktav Publishing House & Anti-Defamation League of
B'nai B'rith, 1975.

Koltun, E. (ed.). *The Jewish woman: New perspectives.* New York:
Schocken Books, 1976.

Kubler-Ross, E. *On death and dying.* New York: MacMillan,
1970.

Lerner, A. *The movement for equal rights for women in American
Jewry.* New York: American Jewish Committee, 1977.

Leventhal, H., J. Watts & F. Pagano. Effects of fear and instruc-
tions on how to cope with danger. *Journal of Personality and
Social Psychology,* 1967, 6, 313-321.

Longworth, P. (ed.) *Confrontations with Judaism.* London,
England: Anthony Blond Ltd., 1966.

Lynch, J. *The broken heart: The medical consequences of loneliness.*
New York: Basic Books, 1977.

Maimonides, M. *The guide for the perplexed* (M. Friendlander,
trans.). New York: Dover, 1904.

— Mishnah Torah (6 Vols.). New York: M.P. Press, 1962.

Maital, S. The tax-evasion virus. *Psychology Today,* March 1982,
16(3), 74-78.

Maslow, A. *Religions, values, and peak experiences.* New York:
Viking Press, 1970.

Massarik, F. *Intermarriage: Facts for planning.* New York:
Council of Jewish Federations and Welfare Funds, no date.

Mead, M. *Male and female: A study of the sexes in a changing
world.* New York: Dell Books, 1968.

— *Can the American family survive?* Redbook, February, 1977, p. 161.

Meerloo, J. *Suicide and mass suicide.* New York, E.P. Dutton, 1968.

Menninger, K. *The vital balance: The life process in mental health and illness.* New York: Viking Press, 1967.

Mekhilta. In *Five Books of the Torah with Malbim Commentary* (6 Vols.). New York: Grossman Publishing, 1964.

Mewborn, C. & R. Rogers. Effects of threatening and reassuring components of fear appeals in physiological and verbal measures of emotion and attitudes. *Journal of Experimental Social Psychology*, 1979, 15, 242-253.

Miale, F. & M. Selzer. *The Nuremberg mind: The psychology of the Nazi leaders.* New York: Quadrangle/The New York Times Book Company, 1975.

Miller, J. (ed.). *Psychoanalysis and women.* Baltimore: Penguin Books, 1973.

Mitchell, J. *Psychoanalysis and feminism.* New York: Random House, 1974.

Montagu, A. *The natural superiority of women.* New York: MacMillan, 1971.

Moustakas, C. *Loneliness.* Englewood Cliffs. New Jersey: Prentice-Hall, 1961.

Mowrer, O. *The crisis in psychiatry and religion.* Princeton: Van Nostrand, 1961.

Nahmanides, M. *Peirush Ramban al ha-Torah.* Jerusalem: Mosad Harav Kuk, 1976.

Nichols, J. *Men's liberation: A new definition of masculinity.* New York: Penguin Books, 1975.

Pines, A., E. Aronson & D. Kafry. *Burnout: From tedium to personal growth.* New York: Free Press, 1981.

Pruyser, P. Is mental health possible? *Bulletin of the Menninger Clinic*, 1958, 22, 58-66.

Rosenthal, T. & B. Zimmerman. *Social learning and cognition.* New York: Academic Press, 1978.

Rosenzweig, F. *On Jewish learning.* New York: Schocken Books, 1955.

Rosner, F. Suicide in Biblical, Talmud, and Rabbinic writings. *Tradition*, 1970, 11(2), 25-40.

Rubenstein, R. Review of "The Nuremberg mind - The psychology of the Nazi leaders." *Psychology Today*, July 1976, 10(2), 83-84.

Rubin, Z. Seeking a cure for loneliness. *Psychology Today*, October 1979, 13(4), 82-90.

Ruitenbeck, H. (ed.). *Death: Interpretations.* New York: Dell Publishing Co., 1969.

Schlesinger, B. Jewish one-parent families: A growing phenomenon in the 1970's. *Journal of Psychology and Judaism*, 1983, 7(2), 89-100.

Seder tefilot mikal hashanah. New York: Kehot Publishing Co., 1965.

Sefer HaHinukh of Aharon of Barcelona (C. Chavel, ed.). Jerusalem: Mosad Harav Kuk, 1957.

Seudfeld, P. Quoted in Rubin, Z. Seeking a cure for loneliness. *Psychology Today*, October 1797, 13(4), 82-90.

Sharot, S. Hasidism and the routinization of charisma. *Journal for the Scientific Study of Religion*, 1980, 19(4), 325-336.

Sheiltot D'rav A'hai Gaon (3 vols.). Jerusalem: Mosad Harav Kuk, 1967.

Sherman, J. *On the psychology of women: A survey of empirical studies.* Springfield, Illinois: Charles C. Thomas, 1971.

Shulhan Arukh (10 vols.). New York: M.P. Press, 1965.

Sifra. In *Five Books of the Torah with Malbim Commentary* (6 vols.). New York: Grossman Publishing, 1964.

Slater, P. *The pursuit of loneliness: American culture at the breaking point.* Boston: Beacon Press, 1970.

Sofer, M. *Responsa* (Vol. 1). New York: Grossman Publishing, 1958.

Spock, B. *Decent and indecent.* Greenwich, Connecticut: Fawcett Publications, 1971.

Stengel, E. *Suicide and attempted suicide.* Middlesex, England: Penguin Books, 1971.

Stevens, C., A. Blank & G. Poushinsky. Religion as a factor in morality reasearch: A cross-sectional analysis of older adolescents, young adults, middle age and senior citizens. *Journal of Psychology and Judaism*, 1977, 1(2), 61-80.

Strouse, J. (ed.). *Women and analysis. Dialogues on psychoanalytic views on femininity.* New York: Viking Press, 1974.

The Talmud (18 Vols). I. Epstein (ed.). London: Soncino Press, 1961.

Thio, A. *Deviant behavior.* Boston. Houghton Mifflin, 1978.

Thompson, C. *On women.* New York: New American Library, 1971.

Tukacinsky, Y. *Gesher HaHayyim* (Vol. 1). Jerusalem: Private Printing, 1960.

Waxman, C. How many are we? Where are we going? *Jewish Life*, Spring-Summer 1982, 6(1), 37-44.

Weiss, R. *Loneliness: The experience of emotional and social isolation.* Cambridge: MIT Press, 1973.
— *Marital Separation.* New York: Basic Books, 1975.

Wright, D. *The psychology of moral behaviour.* Middlesex: England, Penguin Books, 1971.

Yankelovich, D. *New Rules: Searching for self-fulfillment in a world turned upside-down.* New York: Random House, 1981.

INDEX